GROWN-UP STUFF FOR DUMMIES

Some Thoughts for Being an Adult in C21

DAVID NORTON

PAGE PUBLISHING, INC.
New York, NY

First originally published by Page Publishing, Inc. 2019

ISBN 978-1-64424-872-0 (Paperback)
ISBN 978-1-64424-873-7 (Digital)

Printed in the United States of America

Commandments and Clichés

- Keep it simple stupid.
- The Salvation Army is the only free lunch.
- *Festina lente*—hurry slowly.
- If you feel sorry for yourself no one else needs to bother.
- Choose your friends with care.
- Do not make enemies.
- If you cannot afford it do not buy it.
- Mean it even if you don't.
- Measure twice, cut once.
- Take time to smell the roses.
- "To thine own self be true."
- Create something.
- If it seems too good to be true it is.
- Do not ask questions if you do not want the answer.
- Others may be too smart or too stupid to control.
- Stay in control of yourself.
- Give moderation a chance.
- Do it, but do not bore others with the telling of it.
- If it's important, sleep on it (decision or squeeze).
- "Everyone does it." *Never* think you are everyone.
- Fifty percent of people are below average.
- Get over it.
- It is never as good or as bad as "they" say it is or will be.

The rest is simple.

In Sickness and…in Wealth for the Medics

Time was that if you were ill a doctor came to your house in his car with his bag. He told you to stay in bed for one day after your temperature was normal. You felt better soon or not.

Today you must go to a surgery, a misnomer; no surgeon is present, no *ectomy* performed.

Medical Procedure

You go to this surgery, where you sit with a lot of sick people and watch time tick past your appointment.

The doctor finishes doing personal stuff; he runs his hands over you like a soft-core gay movie. Then his squeezes (her name is Nurse) books you in for the next week to confirm you are ill.

If she cannot guess what is wrong with you an appointment is made for you with a "specialist" who majored summa cum laude in billing.

You get better or not. Now it just takes more time and money.

Treatment

Do NOT take drugs unless absolutely necessary and you know what they are.

Do NOT take part in experimental tests or courses unless you do litigation instead of macramé or stamp collecting.

Pay up and smile.

Termination

If the bod or the brain wants to pack it in, the medics morph into a soccer-like team and take the game of you into "time added on."

For six weeks of "injury time" the afflicted lies prone in an uncomfortable bed, unable to speak, and watches the nearest and dearest hogging the grapes and discussing spring daffodil allergy, or the duty nurse's rack.

Then God blows the whistle. He's been watching, complaining to Hippocrates and Old Father Tyme and feeding Storky-Treats to a big white bird (on hand for those who fancy Reincarnation).

Solution

Stay well, do not take bodily risks, get good insurance, and find a doctor who can tell the time.

Do not ask me how I am. I am always very well.
(Headmistress of top English girls' school)

Sunburn

Some people have skin that burns more quickly than a glance of passion on a fast-moving escalator. Others can sit in the sun all day and look like Cleopatra tarted up for Julius Caesar. It really is the luck of the draw.

If you have a skin like a Tide commercial and you overdo it on the beach, you do not need fortissimo: "Oooh you are red! Bet that hurts."

Do not be on either end of that.

Yes, it does hurt. No it's not pretty, and you feel like hell, and embarrassed. No. It will not be any better in the morning. It will take at least two days during which you will feel and look like a lemon.

Would you say to the guy in shorts with the tin leg "Why don't you try for *Strictly Come Dancing?*" It's just about as offensive.

A word of comfort for the palefaces. More than one girl who fancied a frolic with her ski instructor—the one with the deep tan, the ski mask on the forehead and the P&G smile. When it came to bedtime it turned out that the tan finished where he finished shaving and the rest was white as the driven snow and not much else to. Oh never mind.

Pills

Pills fall into three categories—placebos, addictive, and stuff you buy in the Purple Pussycat or the next street corner. Doctors will insist one of the first two, because there is no profit in the third. Placebos often do more good than either of the others.

Hypochondria
DON'T

Molière's *Malade Imaginaire* was not the first hypochondriac, and the millennial frantic about his nicotine stained toenails will not be the last.

Security blanket perhaps; self-absorption almost certainly; fear of death, quite likely; bad potty training, unlikely.

You want an expensive hobby? Instead of hypochondria, start collecting Bentleys. Cheaper and you may get a return on your money.

If you find yourself with even early symptoms of hypochondria, just remember only two things in life are inevitable.

You Only Get One Bod so Take Care of It

Dental

The candlelight, the soft music, and you both know exactly what is going to happen next. Tonight's the night! So to finish off the evening, you share a caramel-based raspberry sticky cake. You look into each other's eyes and feed each other a spoonful. And then you have to clench the upper set to the lower.

Of course you may get lucky until the next morning and you go into the host bathroom: There is the smile that looked so good in the candlelight—in a glass all by itself. Time to call Uber.

It may hurt but go to the dentist. Your teeth do not last as long as the rest of the bod and dental treatment and the cost get more painful as the years roll by.

Much dental insurance varies from suspect to "Forget it. Do not bother."

In the old days in the north of England the miner's wives used to go to the dentist once—the day after the wedding. The snappers had caught their prey and had no further purpose.

Personal hygiene

Not everything about the modern urban world is wonderful but toothpaste and a regular shower or bath rate fairly high. Apparently they had to cut off the clothes of Good Queen Bess due to not washing behind the ears and elsewhere. No wonder she died The Virgin Queen.

The Australians use the simile "dry as a Pommie's towel," but fortunately the days are almost over when the English bathtub doubled as a kitchen counter or used to store coal. (Strange, but true.)

Adopt the water-all-over-the-bod daily habit—not just "pits and parts." A health note: funny how the dandruff storm seems to recede with a daily shampoo even with washing up liquid.

If the *H* in "Hi" or "Can I help you?" brings with it a cheery reminder of street hotdog onions, you are off to a poor start in friendship, love or business.

Every retailer should offer free mouthwash as well as hand sanitizer to all staff.

Personal Exercise

- It is boring so listen to musicradio news or readings from the Koran in Swedish.
- It can disrupt your day so plan for it.
- You may meet those who are fitter stronger thinner or just as likely, flabbier weaker and fatter.
- Stop whining and do it.

There are some wrong ideas about exercise.

- The overmuscled bod is NOT a guarantee of a life of wild sex. Plenty find it a major turn off. The biceps of a weight lifting youth may well herald bingo flab for the future.

- It may help, but trying to morph into a gym rat is not a shortcut to the end of the beer gut. For that, cut out "one (or more) for the road."
- You do not need to do more exercise today than yesterday.
- You do not need to be a prig or an evangelist. Although you may lead by example there is no need to preach. No one wants to hear about the inner joy standing on one foot can bring you, or that man can live on yoga and yoghurt alone.
- To prefer a life of indolence and potential chest pain is a matter of choice and none of your damn business.

Exercise does not mean you must limp round twenty-six miles of marathon hell, nor do you have to become a vegan or a twelve-stepper. On the other hand exercise actually does make you feel better and can give a nice smug feeling.

Bingo flab—the upper arms of those of a certain age seen when they raise a hand as they shout BINGO.

Money Makes the World Go Round

(Just make sure it is *your* world.)

Money is simple:

1. Earn it or better, inherit it. Do NOT steal it. It is just not worth the candle. Ask Bernie Madoff.
2. Do NOT lend, give. You are more likely to get it back.
3. Do NOT borrow. House owners who have a mortgage spend double the sticker price.
4. Save what you can as soon as you can. Let someone pay YOU interest, not vice versa.
5. Build up a reserve fund until you have enough for at least six months.
6. Save and compound. The interest you earn will amaze you.
7. Do NOT discuss it with any but your very nearest and dearest, and even then be on the Qui Vive
8. Do NOT joke about it, because no one gets it.
9. Do NOT lie about it. You will be found out.
10. Do NOT spend what you do not have. (See no. 3 above.)
11. Beware of "financial advisers." There are some good ones, and there are the others.

12. Stand your round in the bar and in life; but do not be flash, because you will look like an idiot, impress no one.

Remember, "investors" (and gamblers) will always tell you their successes, rarely their failures. A financial consultant needs his advice more than you do, even if he works for a bank or perhaps particularly if he does.

Do not try to keep up with the Jones family, who are probably going broke.

Money can turn normal beings into monsters permanently.

Charity

At best one of the good bits of human nature. At worst a most despicable kind of theft. Without doubt the most giving are the least noticed. You hear less about work by Doctors Without Borders than you do about Plastic Surgeons on Palm Beach.

At most natural or manmade disasters first on the scene is the Salvation Army.

So think twice before you give, where you give, how you give and to whom you give.

Hard-hearted?

1. It is likely the homeless person into whose hand you thrust your conscience contribution regards you with contempt.
2. To be registered a charity may need to give just one dollar, yen, pound or euro to the cause. What remains may be used for "administrative" expenses.
3. The first to reach lottery winners are the TV ministries.

4. Churches in Spain have statues of the Virgin Mary with hands upraised and fingers spread. Each finger holds rings, mainly gold and precious stone donated over the years by the women of the Pueblo.
5. There are many corporations who "suggest" their employees agree to have deducted at source a contribution to a charity chosen by the BoD.

If everyone really believed 'Charity begins at home' it would change the tax laws forever.
(**Anonymous tax lawyer**)

Credit Cards

In this day and age we live and quite literally die on our credit cards. So unless you are working as a laborer on a kale plantation in Tierra del Fuego you need a credit card.

Today, very few think you are Jack the Lad if you pull out a wallet full of engraved plastic. It can actually raise suspicion.

Use one card and have one as a spare, because there are places that do not take all cards. K.I.S.S.

A pink, yellow, mauve, gold, silver, platinum, or titanium card issued by the Jute Bank of Iceland has no added value. The one card you might like is black, and you will not be getting one of those anytime soon.

Stick with the majors, and even so before you sign up make sure you know both sides of the bargain (which it is not).

Keep a record of the number and password of all cards, but NOT in your wallet or handbag. Put them, without names or details, on the back of an envelope, which you hide under the fish knives you never use, but memorize them first.

Do NOT put the numbers on your telephone unless they are disguised as Fifi's telephone number, or how much you might win on an accumulator bet for Thursday's card at Gulf Stream Park.

If in any way your card is lost, stolen or compromised before you draw breath inform the company. They want you to keep on spending, so you will get a new one almost at once.

It is a good idea in all events to replace your card at least once a year. There are too many scams out there to count. Even if this is not perfect protection, it helps.

Be very careful using your card for online purchasing. With Amazon, Apple etc. buy gift cards. For the unknown, particularly overseas don't. Just stay away. The product is likely naff, and the risk enormous.

Study your CC bill. Carefully. If you see something that does not jive, control the damage and call the credit card company. NOW. Do not bother the cops, who are too busy with parking tickets and safeguarding film stars. The FBI are in court.

PAY THE BILL NOW. The CC companies lead a luxury life on the interest for not even very late payments. Pay now, live later.

Bad things happens to those who do not pay. Perhaps you are on the town before a night of wild sex until you watch your card being—quite legally—destroyed at the order of the CC company. It happens—that would be the card destruction, not the wild sex.

Do NOT be suckered into card purchase by offers of a free retro electric toaster or clockwork laptop.

Do NOT accept the offer of a retailer credit card and 50 percent off your long underwear if you…"just sign here please." Break your wrist, froth at the mouth, sing Oh Mammy in the key of D.

Just do not sign. You are dealing here with the masters of fine print. You may even find they were just kidding about the 50 percent discount.

Collections

The *collectors* have nothing to do with the smiling faces who sold you the card in the first place. The collectors go to unarmed combat courses at the weekend, have a knuckle duster in the wallet, a bike chain in the car, and do not do jokes or excuses.

It is no wonder lawyers give their inboard-outboard Seaspeed high-performance speedboats names like Visa or Late Fees.

Expenses

Business Traveling

There is only one way to avoid cheating or losing on travel expenses. It's called a per diem.

Unless you are a anal-retentive and not doing the job you should be doing, it is well-nigh impossible and very boring to keep track of every cent on a business trip. With a reasonable per diem you can eat at McDonalds and save, or dine at the Ritz and pay the difference.

If you're given a briefcase full of travelers checks, justify asap. It will make you feel better and calm those who might be suspicious or jealous.

If you are doing everything on credit cards do it with care. Keep a record and receipts, and do NOT confuse it with personal stuff.

Entertaining

However legitimate it may be, if you submit a bill from the Purple Pussycat featuring four bottles of vintage champagne and ten sticky cocktails, it will raise a red flag. Remember you are as like as not presenting it to someone who caught the 5.39 home, found his dinner in the oven, because his wife had gone to Bingo, and the kids were fighting over the TV remote.

Factoid: The man who invented IKEA didn't. The directors of Walmart don't. So who are all those people who turn left when they board a flight? They can't all be on an upgrade.

Borrowing and Lending

William Shakespeare (whoever he was/they were) knew a thing or two. Polonius, father to Hamlet's squeeze, is right: "Neither a borrower nor a lender be."

Lending

If you lend do not expect it back. Your favorite book, the twenty in the pub, your best shirt, eyeliner, dress, old school tie—forget it. Do not keep asking for it back; that is the rock on which many a friendship has foundered. It's your fault. If you wanted to keep it you should never have lent it. Get over it.

Your car you will get back—with no petrol, a parking ticket, a key scratch—all to variations of: "Oh really? Are you sure?"

Just be grateful to see any loan returned. Don't like the odds? Don't lend.

Borrowing

"I do not owe anyone anything."

Really? No mortgage? No car payments? No little loan/overdraft at the bank? Credit cards all paid up?

Individuals, like nations and corporations, frequently stare bankruptcy in the face. Banks, credit card companies and other lenders never do.

Before you take out the mortgage on that smart riverside home or sign the down payment on the boy racer Ferrari, work out how much it will REALLY cost you.

Do NOT borrow socially even on a small scale. If for some reason you do, return the loan asap without request, fuss or nonsense. Repeated reference gets very tired and does NOT settle the loan.

Do not go the "forgotten-wallet" route. You will look mean, devious and dishonest. If it happens to be true, and it sometimes is, host the next occasion at twice the price. Unfair? Look on it as the cost of doing business.

Gambling

Gambling is fun, and that is exactly what it is. Whatever you have seen or read that is all it is—FUN.

Do not even think you are going to make a fortune at a green table wearing an eyeshade or day trading on the markets.

The small time "investor" will always tell you about the killing he made buying Apple as a penny stock. Somehow he glosses over the packet he lost on Enron or Carillion, or the absolute certainty given to him by the girlfriend of the cousin of the barman.

You will never break the bank at Monte Carlo or Las Vegas.

Occasionally a gambler will get on a lucky streak, find how to count cards, or something similar. The casinos are watching. That glittery ceiling above the table conceals a battery of cameras and an army of watchers.

It does happen that there is a genuine run of luck combined with skill. In such cases the casino will send luxury cars or airplanes, give free everything in case he takes his luck elsewhere. As usual the casino wins.

Slot machines? The casino owns the machines. Do the math.

A day at the races is much more fun, but the man who leaves with the most money is the bookie on the rails.

Never bet on anything you do not understand or cannot play. Beginners luck is one of the world's biggest lies. For example there are those who pretend myopia, but can in fact go round the dart board with six inch nails. (Also watch PaulNewman in The Hustler).

Yes having a go is fun. Enjoy, have a blast, but set a limit. If you cannot do that, stop at once and seek help. Seriously.

Contracts and Lawyers

Contracts

> I am creative. I live for my art, a citizen of the planet, and cannot be ruled by trivial paperwork. Mr. Creative Van Gogh–in–waiting. Get over it and pay attention.

At least two things are wrong with this statement:

1. No one is creative if they say they are.
2. All are subject to contracts of one sort or another.

Contracts are something new? Refer to Shakespeare and *The Merchant of Venice*—sixteenth century.

It may be a lease on a car, a family home, an agent getting his cut, or rebuilding the Pyramids or repainting the Vatican.

You can make a contract on a handshake, but beware of warm cuddly agreements with family or friends. If it is a friend you may lose him. If it is not a friend you may lose everything. If it's family you may be cut out of the will.

If in doubt which you probably are, consult a lawyer. Contracts, not TV court drama, are why lawyers get the big bucks.

1. "Read the contract" makes no sense today unless you are an anally retentive lawyer wannabe. If you buy an app or new telephone etc., it is suggested you read six pages of fine print put together by lawyers closing on five-bedroom ocean front villas. Thus the document has to be offered to the punter, or they might be sued by other lawyers. The fact that less than one (a lawyer) in one million reads it is irrelevant. The CYA has been taken.

2. You need to consult a lawyer because contracts can get very creative—that's why. Not only do lawyers read them, they write them. They speak legalese, so they understand them.

3. If you and/or your lawyer do not like what is on offer, do not accept. Contracts are almost always in favor of the writer.

4. "It's our standard contract. Everyone signs it." Wrong! *Never, no how nowhere think you are everyone.* A contract between honest people can go well or not so well. Like all relationships it may depend on the work you put into it. Make sure there is a very clear paragraph about noncompliance which everyone agrees.

5. Understand and agree the money involved. Then *quietly* put aside a contingency. Ten percent is a good guide. Do not tell the contractor, because he will find a way to spend it. It may well get eaten, because such is life. If it does not, you will have saved some money.

The rock musician who put into his contract that he wanted only green M&M's in his dressing room was not being a dork. He wanted to see if the lawyers read the contract. Smart rocker, at least one smart lawyer.

Lawyers

1. Never use the cousin of the potential squeeze who promised a quid pro quo. When you need a lawyer, spend the money and get the best. First agree to his rate while working with him. Make absolutely certain he does not charge you while he tells you the one about the gay Mongolian nun. Funny how many jokes lawyers know.
2. A good lawyer will always tell you to stay out of the courts if you possibly can. HE IS RIGHT.
3. Befriend a lawyer. God knows they need friends, and it's good to be able to get *simple* advice in the pub, not in the office at $500 an hour.

There are two ways to get difficult things done. Agree first or apologize after. (**Ron Shay**) attrib.

Last Will and Testament

Make a will. If you do not, you may well regret it in the afterlife if not before. Keep it up to date. Do not discuss it. Do not use it as a weapon.

*"I, E**z* M****n, being out sound mind, (Ha Ha Ha)"* **True first line of Will**

Love, Pain and the Whole Damn Thing

Entry

Despite innumerable inaccurate handbooks, songs, blind dates, friendly advice "No Fail" dating services blurb, not to mention your mother, the love thing just happens.

Very few get it right on Take One or Two, so do not panic.

So where do we go to find love in the city or the country, or even suburbia?

School

School days school days
Good ol' golden rule days
Reading, writing, 'rithmetic,
Taught to the tune of the hickory stick
You were my queen in Calico
I was your barefoot bashful beau
And you wrote on my slate 'I love you Joe'
When we were a couple of kids.

That was 1907, so there are a few changes, but you get the general idea. Requires a lot of stamina and might be a bit limiting. Best to put in time between sixth grade and seduction.

Family

First rule: Mother does NOT know best.

Second rule: Father is not much better.

"He's the richest foot doctor not in *Strictly Come Dancing*!" Those hands know dark secrets. *Thanks but no thanks.*

"But they are such a happy family!" Long may they stay as such. *You hope to start one not join one.*

"Looks aren't everything!" *No, but they are something.*

Legend has it that the daughter of a famous underwear designer retained her virginity because at the moment of truth, she would see her father's name just above the command center.

Work or Work-Related

A very popular option with pitfalls. Sandra from accounts payable may have great pair of knockers, but she may also be the office bicycle. Brian with the Harley-Davidson, Gucci shades and killer smile, may be the company center for diseases, not all of which react to penicillin.

If the hormones rage and interrupt the work day, KEEP IT QUIET, and more important, OFF the premises. You are in a fishbowl, so everyone can see, and not all of them are your friends.

Are you sharing lust with the CFO?

Did Sandra get knocked up after the Christmas party, and now needs a husband PDQ because Jason who dunnit, was fired.

Is Mandy looking for someone to break up her marriage before she leaves for San Francisco with a transgender bodybuilder?

A work place break up can bring disaster. There is no joy in having to explain in a client meeting why SHE is weeping like a Victorian melodrama, or how HE has spilt his coffee on your presentation.

This is often the moment everyone may pick sides and they will.

None of this stops the workplace from being a good option.

Holiday or Shipboard Romance

The cruise holiday romance was great while it lasted for De Caprio and Winslett on the *Titanic*. Unfortunately, or perhaps luckily they did not live to see how it might have panned out.

Holding hands as the sun sinks slowly into the Caribbean or even behind the English pub in Torremolinos is not the same as karaoke night at the local, or the apartment with the unwashed coffee cups.

Not to say romantic transfer is impossible, but it is probably better not to propose undying love until you have had a couple of test drives on familiar roads on dry land.

Church, Synagogue, Golf Club, Football, Supermarket or other Holy Temple

Very good as long as you are a true believer, not just there for entertainment. In that case you could be on a loser.

Warning: You may be influenced by the rest of the congregation, family, fans, or shoppers.

Lonely Hearts et. al.

A growing niche industry, and nothing wrong with it. Those who like it say it has a huge (if unproven) success rate. Others say it is how desperate people meet other desperate people. A matter of choice, but a deliberate choice it is.

All of the above—and others—may work, but they all require…*chance.*

Chance means luck, and getting it right requires plenty of that. It may not always seem it is in favor of the deserving.

> *Chance would be a fine thing.* (**Anna Menzies**)
> - attrib

Exit

Divorce may be a legal thing, or just a "Dear John" after a brief emotional error of judgment. The same rules apply.

There are plenty out there with soothing feel-good advice, and a lot of professional and amateur marriage counselors. BEWARE!

Take your choice of the reason. Incompatibility, in-laws, incompetence, incontinence, inconvenience, innocence and there are a thousand more.

There is always enough blame/responsibility for everyone to share. The truth is there was a lack wit or wisdom—probably quite early on, and eventually that gets like an old set of Michelins not worth patching.

In almost every failed relationship someone takes the moral high ground, and often everyone does. That is a load of guano.

Why does she have wild sex with the pizza delivery boy? Because she is not getting what she wanted. She should have made this clear before "I do." Or certainly before it came to this. Why does he get drunk with the single people at the office? Because he is bored to death at home and should have done something to change it a long time ago. Etc. etc. It happens. The whole thing is a mess.

First decide if you want to make it work. If so talk it through. Are you sure it is what you mean? Do you realize you are giving up a lot of history, private jokes and, yes, love? Are you quite sure the hyena-like laugh of your new-found love will not drive you crazy six months from now? You have mentally measured at least twice? Okay. Cut once and at once. The worst thing for everyone is to let it drift on and on and on. It will get worse not better. The longer this has been going on the more drastically your life will change. The failure may seem to be one-sided, but it is not. The surgery is painful, guilt-ridden and depressing. The more so the longer the relationship.

Two bad things about divorce—the cost and the kids. Two may not be able to live as cheaply as one, but two apart is more expensive.

One of the saddest city sights is the weekend father, trying to find fun things to do with two little strangers, who would rather be at home or playing with their mates.

Do NOT on any account share a lawyer.

Be absolutely sure of your agreement.

Do NOT be fooled by the one-dollar-a-year alimony. A lawyer—yours, not your significant ex other's—will explain this.

Try and keep it simple and civil. Stop sucking your thumb—it is possible.

Sadly (but sometimes happily) you will lose some friends. The d-word heralds an ugly picking of sides.

That's the bad news, but there is some good if you play your cards right and have a bit of luck.

The kids are not having to watch a knockdown parental drag-out fight anymore, or even endure the silence at the dinner table. Yes children DO pick up on these things.

You are not having to pretend a lot of stuff both for yourself and the immediate families, or live a lie in other ways.

You find who your friends are—surprising and illuminating.

Accept passing sympathy and perhaps the odd blind date. No one has the full story, so stay away from well-meant advice. You may well lose as a friend the shoulder you cried on; sad but true.

Do not give a dissertation on the last ten years even if asked. Besides the fact that it can be mind-numbingly boring, it is none of their damn business. So have some strength and dignity.

PLEASE do not play the poor-me card.

Divorce may be the only legal necessary and expensive way, but a lot of the same stuff may apply to LTR or even STR after emotional errors of judgment.

Making Out in Public

Time was in the dim distant past of the latter half of the twentieth century when making out in public was okay and, for a short time in the so-called "sexual revolution," even cool. In some cinemas they removed every other arm rest in the seats at the back.

Today, not so much. Onlookers find it boring, embarrassing, intrusive, and offensive. The epithet "Get a room" is not a hint, it's an insult. The heartfelt kiss and hug of greeting or farewell is fine, late night in the clubs, have at it. Remember, it can be construed as a commitment you had no intention of making.

Otherwise keep the groping for later. It will be more fun, and you can be more expressive.

"I Love You" Dos and Don'ts

"I love you" is a genie that takes time, energy, heartache, respect and even money to stuff back in the bottle. So think very carefully before you take out that particular cork.

It is a biological fact that a man is born with a brain and a penis. Many believe he is not born with enough blood to service both at the same time.

- Do not use "I love you" as a short cut to the bedroom. As with many shortcuts you can get very lost. It may change the contraception guidelines and will likely move the goalposts;
- DO NOT USE "I love you" as a "Get out of jail free" card. This is an old trick used in desperation or ultimatum. Handle with care.

Never, ever, profess love to two people at the same time. All kinds of reasons:

- It can get very confusing.
- People talk, particularly about love, and you could find TWO unhappy people waiting for you when you get home from the pub, the massage parlor, the spa, the date with the hunk/bombshell from accounts payable.
- You may easily find yourself having to meet two sets of potential in-laws, and that is at least one too many.
- You are certainly telling at least one person a whopper.

Roses are red
Violets are blue
I've just slept with…guess who!
(**Rosemary Dulac "Rosemary Remembers"**)

Some Sexual Mores

- Do NOT kiss and tell—well not for at least ten years. Sooner than that it can bite you.
- Do NOT sleep with a virgin unless you really mean it, or you are not given the option. (Some find virginity a bore or a burden and you may be chosen to override it. Bed with care!)
- Do NOT sleep with anyone for a bet. That is about as tacky as you can get.
- If you are questioned on any sexual success or failure smile, look reminiscent or mysterious, sigh (optional), and say: "That is for me to know and not for you to ask."

Do not tell tales about others. You may wonder why the research chemist and the blonde receptionist with the great legs always arrive at work together; they may be neighbors and carpool. If you spot Cyril the CFO coming got out of the Bates Motel with Sandra from accounts payable and looking furtive, tell yourself they have been doing research on a dodgy customer.

If a name comes up in conversation and you feel the liaison needs airing and sharing, do not go tabloid. A raised eyebrow, the mysterious look, and perhaps "Hmmmmm" should do the trick whilst leaving you blameless—almost.

If you can't be good, be careful. If you can't be careful at least remember the day of the month.
(**WRN**)

Weddings

Encouraged by Hallmark Cards et. al., there are many who believe a woman's life is worth nothing if her parents do not go broke throwing a wedding.

You may have heard the expression "spare prick at a wedding." This refers to the bridegroom. Bridezilla may define not only the bride, but any woman involved.

If the father of the bride has the sense to offer cash in lieu ACCEPT the registry office. Although you may miss out on the toasters and a print of *Monarch of the Glen*, the bride will not need white meringue which looks great from the back, and the groom stands a much better chance of getting on with his father-in-law, because they can afford two rounds at the pub, Cup Final final tickets, or an obvious ten-spot in the church collection.

She: Is there a doctor in the house! Is there a
doctor in the house!
He: Yes madam, can I help? I am a doctor.
She: Oh boy! Have I got a daughter for you?

Adultery

Adultery can sometimes be very tempting. Many fall into that deep dark well prompted by the long, heartfelt conversation that includes: "My (*significant other*) does not understand me my dog, my mother, my pet pig. But *you* are so sensitive." *Uh huh.* Or: "We have an open marriage." *And you both agree on this?* Or: "I knew just looking at you there was something special between us." *Was it that obvious? I should have worn a bra or looser pants.*

And there are plenty more.

Adultery pillow talk may turn out to be boring and/or expensive. It may concern the spouse, the children, the bank account, the in-laws, a comparison and critique of your technique, which may become a subject of discussion with friends—or worse—family.

The post pillow talk may be perilous: "Oh silly me! I forgot to take the pill."

Or: (*Not so bad, but not good for the self-esteem*) "What was your name again?"

Or: "You don't get out much, do you?"

And then:

"I have had a chat with your wife/husband. He/she wishes us all the best, and can you call his/her lawyer about the court date."

"I have not had a chat with your wife/husband. Yet. Make the check out to cash."

"I don't care what I said then, and I do not care what you may feel, or that you called your ex-dearly-beloved to say you have at last found your life partner. I have NOT fallen in love with you."

"He/she is suspicious and is coming around to your place after the bodybuilding workout. I hid the pistol, but he/she often carries a switchblade. Call me later if possible."

"I want you to come and see the cutest little apartment I've found for us. It is a little bit pricey, but it does have four bedrooms and a separate sitting room for Nanny."

"They say it's going to be a boy. I wonder if he'll look like you."

Fatal Attraction may be an old movie but it is a must see for any potential adulterer. Sometimes adultery does work out. Just make absolutely damn sure you mean it, because if you have got it wrong the next chapter can be disastrous, disruptive and expensive.

You, Me, and Him or Her

The eternal triangle can be good fun to watch in movies. In real life not so much. The third spoke is however not necessarily the lover past, present or future. It can be the parent, the priest (rabbi), the sibling, the boss, the (step) child—to name but a few.

He/she may be lust come to life. If you see three is company run like hell. It will only get worse. References? There are plenty.

> *There are three people in this marriage.* (**Diana, Princess of Wales**)

Rent, Buy or Sofa Surf?

SOFA SURF

Homelessness can happen in a variety of ways; it gets tired very quickly. You may not fancy going back to the parents and the little room where you had your teenage fantasies of greatness and girls/guys, but it is a LOT better than the alternative, which is the back of the car, the all-night caff/public transport.

Sofa surfing is the next step up. It is almost a Rite of Passage, but is a top five way to lose friends. This is not quite the same as waking up in a strange bed after whatever…, but most of the same rules apply.

To avoid a change of lock on the door of the nest where you are playing cuckoo, make your footprint as small as possible.

- Do not hog the bathroom at morning rush hour.
- Toothpaste razor etc. are not community property.
- Do not hit on the host's spouse/significant other.
- Do not snoop. That includes computer.
- Do not bring back drunk mates from the pub/office.
- Put more back in the fridge than you take out.
- If you meet casual hookup or even the love of your life arrange an away fixture.
- Spend as much time out as possible, but do not come back late and drunk without a key.

- Surf the sofa as short a time as possible.
- Do not take sides in domestic affairs.
- BE TIDY AND CLEAN.

Do NOT make a habit of it. Word gets around.

Having done the sofa circuit, and you probably will, you might try and shack up with a deaf and dumb nymphomaniac who owns a pub on a golf course. If that does not work out for some reason you have two options.

RENT OR BUY?

Some things apply to both.

- The price is too high, but both sides know that.
- The blonde property "expert" in the too tight black HC trouser suit is the promoted (or demoted) cousin of the pepsodent smile at the car dealership. Both survive on a diet of quasi-friendship and are no more your friend than a waiter.
- Do NOT listen to story about six people ready to snap it up, but you were first. Often used, it is on the biggest lies list.
- Read all documentation with care. Then give it to a lawyer.
- Location. Is it under the flight path, next to the local nick, saw mill, school or power station; the sexy neighbor may have a spouse, three children under the age of five, and a large gun collection.
- Location. Has it got the things *you* need—shops, schools, libraries, church, synagogue, art gallery, and massage parlor?

- Location. How difficult is it to travel to the above, AND the airport, the ocean, the gym, the significant other, and most important, where you go to earn the scratch to pay for it?

Rent

No capital investment, shirking responsibility, not being able to fully adapt your living space to your needs, the landlord has you by the short hairs, you have no security beyond your lease, you may ask for repairs which may never get done etc., etc.

All true. On the other hand

- you can see if you like the district, country or city of choice before you make what may be the wrong commitment;
- no need to maintain—very important for travelers;
- no resale when you want to move on;
- no need reorganize when you suddenly have to support a dog, spouse, peacock, parrot, pig, or parent;
- your lifestyle or ambition might not favor a mortgage or all of the money left you by your (not-so) rich aunt.

Buy

There are all the good things the blonde "property expert" (see above) will tell you. For example you may "need" not to fall behind as property values go up. This is likely to be true long term, but sometimes VERY long term. (She did not bother to remind you of the hefty whack she will make out of your decision.)

Why pay someone else when you could be making an "investment?"

Fare's Fair
(But it depends on the chef.)

RESTAURANTS

The reasons for going to restaurants are

- laziness
- lack of time
- "I don't know how to boil an egg."
- wanting to impress (often related to leg over),
- a craving for Indian, Chinese, or North Bulgarian dumplings.

Never go to an empty restaurant unless you know it well and are first there. The service of the disillusioned waiter and last week's microwaved food will have driven away even the most optimistic.

Large restaurants are frequently empty because there is no atmosphere and they are paying too much rent/mortgage, which is being passed on to the luckless diner. *There are of course a few exceptions, the best known being La Coupole in Paris. This is about the size of a league two football ground. The service is amazing, the food good (real) French, and the other diners are fascinating.*

Never go to the restaurant of the moment unless you know the owner really well and want to impress. The service may well be sketchy and the food worse.

The restaurant that you and your smart friends raved about before Christmas may have had two new chefs and a failed health inspection by Easter.

Never ever go to a restaurant where the menu is over a page long. If you must go, check the microwave because that is whence your food will leave the "kitchen."

Always go to a gala opening as long as it's free.

Unless one wealthy and foolish patron of gastronomy is footing the bill, NEVER be in a party of more than six, and four is better. The conversation at the table will divide and the one on the other end of the table will be far more interesting than yours.

Waiters cannot count much over five, and do not have room on that silly little notebook for more orders anyway.

Avoid a table in the middle of the restaurant (elbow jogging) or the front door (draughty). Do not accept a table next to the service door unless you enjoy the clash of trays and are a student of Tunisian patois or Serbo-Croat cursing.

If you are two, try and eat at the bar. Service is just as good, and you may miss the joy of neighboring tables behind bussed.

Do not be put down or intimidated by the maître d'. He lives (very nicely thank you) on being overtipped. He does not need your money any more than does the doorman at the Plaza.

PLEASE do not engage in lengthy conversation about whether the French beans came from France, or instructions on how to cook the spaghetti noodles. The waiter will lie about the former because he has no idea, and ignore the latter because the chef will throw food at him. These are the facts. This nonsense impresses no one and can embarrass everyone. If you are not the host it is really bad manners.

If the food is really too awful to eat do NOT send it back. Leave it and stop at the local Greasy Spoon on the way home. If your almost untouched plate is challenged, wet your napkin, hold it to your head, and say you could taste powdered dry quince to which you are highly allergic.

Don't order the most expensive thing on the menu unless invited.

Do not go to an Indian restaurant and order an omelet and chips. Do not go to a steak restaurant and ask to see the vegan menu. You ask "Why not?" Don't ask.

Best advice: Find a significant other who can cook, or take a Cordon Bleu course yourself, and stay at home.

Your Waiter Is Not Your Friend

- The work is not well paid, the hours unsocial, the kitchen staff frequently unpleasant, uncooperative and jealous of the tips although they earn more.
- The role of the waiter is to take the order right, bring what was ordered before the sauce resembles tractor grease, and disappear until it's time for the next course or the bill.
- His first name, political views and family snaps are intrusive and equate to bad service. The diner does not need a rundown on kitchen politics or how badly everyone tips.
- Always check the "service compris" The waiter is not going to tell you.

"I've Got a Great Idea...!"

You are at a bar, beach, picnic, party, and having a great time. For whatever reason it is time to move on. (This is often soon after the sun goes down). Someone suggests "We all go on to that fab place in the Kings Road. The owner is an old pal! He'll squeeze us in!"

Everyone piles into cars, Ubers, cabs and off you go. You sit down with fifteen people, all of whom have drink taken, and none of whom you really know. The gorgeous and witty one with whom you thought you were on a promise is at the other end being hit upon.

The waiters may well be at the end of a long shift, but the owner is not going to turn away the money. More (overpriced) booze takes forever to arrive wrong because someone ordered an appletini. By the time the very ordinary wine is dumped at the other end of the table you are completely sober with a sick headache. Nuked food arrives eventually, but is not what you ordered.

When it comes to pay one person has left his wallet in the car and disappears to "fetch it" and another the one who ate all the bread sees no reason why "everyone else pig out when all I had was a salad, which was bloody awful anyway."

No NO NO NO NO NO and NO.

Foods Fads and Diets

Picky eating is the height of bad manners. Parents who allow it should have their children confiscated.

Food is one of the great privileges of life. To deny its delights is pointless and stupid. Simply treat it with the respect it so richly deserves, which, as with just about everything, means in proportion. The only footnote regarding food is respect through skilled cooking.

"If You Eat This Wonderful Diet You Will Live Longer."

Three problems with this:

Do you really want to live the rest of your life on wheat germ, kale roots and tofu? Sounds a lot like slow death by boredom.

In the last fifty years almost every food has been declared by "experts" as both the only path to good health and the road to early mortality.

During two world wars and countless sieges diet was what was available.

Check the longevity of the survivors before championing the "healthy diet."

Yes people do have allergies, a great many of them quite genuine. Then again it is interesting how many people develop allergies to things they do not like.

Obesity is a very sad and either a physical or psychological condition. We can offer no medical solutions or even pretensions thereto. Just great sympathy.

For those that are simply overweight there is one infallible diet: Eat less.

Man is an omnivore. Do not deny the fact—celebrate it. (**Hannibal Lechter**) attrib.

One for the Road

Drink a glass of red wine every day. This will bring physical and mental wellbeing.

As much rubbish as truth is talked mixing drinks, after many many years of research by many it appears to be matter of personal constitution and luck. Sometimes a dram of a twenty-five-year-old single malt followed by a glass of Dom Perignon can cause the major heaves. On the other hand there may be a night on the Retsina with a bottle of Fundador brandy standing by and you wake up ready to run a marathon. Go figure.

With that "very dry martini" forget the "stirred not shaken" rubbish. Just make sure when the smoothie barman has finished shooting his cuffs and throwing the bottles in the air he keeps the top of the Vermouth bottle screwed on. Tight.

Thus you miss the hangover. The late, great **Burt Reynolds**

Wine

Football, sex and wine have one thing in common. They all attract "experts." We have all met the patronizing morons who know it all—sniff the cork, spin the wine glass, bury the bugle in it, spit twice, check the price list and pronounce it "drinkable in a pinch." They have a lexicon of schoolmasterly adjectives such as "cheeky," "amusing," "presumptuous," "ingenuous" or phrases such as "simple in its complexity" or "complex in its simplicity" etc. etc.

In restaurants beware of the sommelier—the one with the silly christening mug round his neck who, uninvited, monopolises the conversation at *your* dinner table with the lexicon of silly words and sillier advice. He might be an actor who cannot even get a gig as the fat man in a TV commercial. Do not have a conversation with him. He is full of it but with better delivery.

Unless you really know what you are doing, downplay. If one of your guests is an expert, real or professed, let him choose. He will be flattered, and if his choice tastes like the Red Sea rather than vin rouge you are off the hook.

If it's left up to you restaurateurs will tell you they sell most of the second cheapest bottle on the list. Just saying.

Getting Drunk

There comes that tipping point. One moment you are in the bar or at the party nice and relaxed and in control; the next the barman has four eyes and you cannot understand why no one is listening to you, which is a good thing because you are talking rubbish.

We nearly all do it at least once. All part of pushing the envelope of youth at whatever age. What you do may be bad. Dancing on the table, swinging on the chandelier, singing "Ave Maria" instead of "Roll over Beethoven" on the karaoke stage, falling asleep with your head in the soup—all those usually become forgotten or dismissed as the folly of youth middle age or senility.

Far worse is what you say. You may say things you swore not to tell. You may say things you do not mean. You may say things you do mean. You may forget and cast aside the joys of contraception. You may think you have at last discovered the meaning of life, which means telling your best friend you are irretrievably, irrevocably in love with his/her spouse, his/her mother/father, or him/her. All can be devastating and can have very ugly consequences.

Hangovers are no fun and take at least half a day out of your life. Alcoholic remorse can take a lifetime.

Do not drink and drive. EVER. In the age of Uber it is unbelievably stupid. It is not only a matter of doing someone harm, which is unforgivable, but also that black SUV you passed on a blind corner may be an unmarked police car.

What happens when you get rear ended on the way home from the pub, and it is not your fault? You get tested anyway.

Even one night in the pokey is no fun, and it gets worse and worse, and more and more expensive.

There is only one thing dumber than driving drunk: texting while driving drunk.

Recreational Drugs

Enough has been written on the subject, but remember a few things.

The odd joint can be the first step down a primrose path. Not necessarily, but possibly. You might not like the places you need to go to find your local retailer, and the sales staff are not your friends. It gets more expensive as time goes by and the thrill gets less the more you seek it until it is too late. What started as a bit of fun with one's peers has ruined the lives and emptied the bank accounts of many. You may find yourself rightly or wrongly in the pokey.

Addiction is horrible at any level. Not preaching. Just saying.

In conclusion get drunk or high if you must. You will. Best advice: do it with the kind of friends who will forgive your peccadillos. Strangers can get very po-faced if you try the technicolor yawn on their Guccis.

Drink is the curse of the working class. (**Karl Marx**)

Work Is the Curse of
the Drinking Class
(Oscar Wilde)

Be Nice to the Novice

The day you start anything is difficult, whether you are taking over as CEO of IBM or the cage opener for the junior branch of the Pigeon Fanciers Club. Everyone seems to know each other and have the whole enchilada down pat.

Fortunately the humiliation of hazing is nearly over, but there are subtler forms of bullying which are just as ugly. On the contrary befriend the lonely, shy one and you may build a worthwhile friendship or alliance.

> *March in step with those on their way up, because you may well pass them again on your waydown.* (**The grand old Duke of York**) (attrib.)

Create Something

If you do not create something you will be replaced or flipping hamburgers—no wait…that too will be soon be AI. You may not think you are much of a painter/writer/sculptor or inventor. How do you know unless you try it, and one thing for sure is that you will get better with practice?

Did you know Jamie Lee Curtis (actress daughter of Tony Curtis and Janet Leigh) invented a patent diaper?

Did you know the work of Hedy Lamarr (mega film star of the 30s) is used in Bluetooth technology TODAY?

Set out to do what you want to do. The eponymous discouraging dumb 'they' could be wrong. It may be less of a leap than THEY told you.

Managing Your Creativity

If you go to a bar or a party or even the office cafeteria and say you are a writer you will find someone who has a brilliant idea for a book he wants you to write.

A few things **wrong** with this scenario:

- He wants 50 percent of your hard work.
- He will think he owns you personally.
- His friend who is a director/agent and publisher is more than likely a myth or at best a one-time leg-over.
- You may find your work gets nicked. It does happen often.
- You may find yourself taken out of the end result.
- It's probably a naff idea anyway.

If you do agree to write, film, paint something ONLY DO IT FOR MONEY.

A few things **right** with this scenario:

- Cash (and deadlines) are the world's greatest incentives for creation.
- Someone thinks you are worthwhile.

- The friend who is a director/agent and publisher is far more likely to exist.
- You have done something right, so you work harder, and do it better.

It may be that one of the greatest playwrights of the last fifty years wrote in a frenzy day and night for the five days before the first read through. Christopher Marlowe had to be dragged out of pub brawls to finish the last act. Jeffrey Barnard, alcohol-based columnist, was frequently "unwell." Van Gogh cut off his ear in frustration or something. Coleridge wrote *Xanadu* with the help of something that would land him in the pokey today. The Who in their prime rearranged hotel rooms.

You are not there yet.

John Grisham started while waiting in between court cases but Brian Jones ended up swimming next to the pool filter. Just saying.

Multitasking

Definition: Doing two things at the same time, both badly.
It is rude and ineffective. Do not do it.
If someone tells you he can, do not trust him. Better still leave, and let him do it by himself.

Politics and Leadership

So you fancy yourself as a village, city, or even a world leader?
If you go all the way, you may get free room and board near or in the office, free hamburgers with president of Basutoland and goat curry with the Imam of Kaffir Ben Delan.

There are lots of photo ops, not all flattering. You may get free car rides with men in dark suits white shirts and deaf aids.

To get anywhere on this rough road you will kiss babies and answer a lot of stupid questions in drafty town halls, and be rewarded by constant abuse.

You had better be married or the media will be on you like flies on raw meat. Do not even consider a freelance knee tremble or even kiss anyone in public after you reach the age of 14, or you will find yourself telling whoppers:

You are almost compelled to award your children state education, where in a good year they will be despised by just under half their contemporaries.

You will have a few geeks and hangers on, but they are all after your job or need a special favor.

When public life is through you may get lucky and publish a book that people will give each other and never read.

Well, as they say, it's a living.

> *Some are born great, some achieve greatness. Some have greatness thrust upon them.* (**Jean Anouilh**)

Being Fired

Believe it or not nearly everyone gets fired at least once and not just the millennial billionaires who then happen upon the app/software no one can live without.

However, whenever, it is a horrible feeling and makes you feel worthless and useless. You are not. You are the same person who woke up that morning, had a cup of coffee, and fed the cat. It will get better. How long that takes is part luck, part timing and the largest part you. Take your head out of the gas oven. Do not panic. Stop feeling sorry for yourself. Do not stick pins in a wax model of the one who did it. If he was out of line…well… God has a way of watching firing very closely. Do not go on a three-day piss up and spend the end of your cash.

None of the above do any good at all. So what do you do?

Tell your Significant Other. There are horrifying tales of pretending to catch the 8.10, but actually spending the day in the pub or the PA's bed. It's the time when you really need all the moral support that's going.

The S.O. may blame, sneer, whine or get a tattoo they (you) can't afford so THEY can feel better. Time to ditch; they probably had it coming anyway. If they are stand up, you have at the least a friend for life, possibly a lot more.

A word of warning. It's a dangerous time for rebound love/ sex. Take all the time you need to decide what you want to do with the rest of your life. Do you love your life as a bean counter, or do you want to run away to Polynesia and paint fat women? Now is the moment to choose.

If you go and see a headhunter take a ONE PAGE resume and follow the interview suggestions below stick as close to the truth as you can, and say what you think you want and will accept. He/she may change it; that is what they do, so be ready to adapt.

If you take the wrong job ONLY because it's offered you will regret it.

It may seem unlikely in those ugly early moments but the vast majority of people in retrospect bless the dismal day of dismissal.

Firing

There are people hired by corporations to fire people. When they have done their number they move on. Not really a calling that needs to be debated here, so moving on.

Unfortunately the act of firing may also be required of us more sensitive little human flowers.

- If it has to be done, do it asap.
- Do not expect: "I hope we can still be friends." Possible but unlikely; certainly not immediately.
- Do it quickly.
- Do not twist the knife, but stick to the (massaged) truth.
- Do not discuss it except perhaps with your significant other unless he/she is in the firing line.
- Only do it for the right reasons. Remember God is watching.

For romantic/sexual firing, follow the above; then…move on.

Office Politics and Partnerships

Make no mistake. If three people are in a room together there is a potential for politics. Three great friends, siblings, cousins or complete strangers. It is amazing how often two side against one.

Politics starts early in our lives. Mommy says no? So we take it to Daddy. No matter how divided it is still two against one, worth the risk to a devious five to ten year old. Once established it can work right through to the full twenty-one and way beyond.

You cannot eliminate the risk of politics, but if you are involved in any partnership social, sexual or professional,

- make sure you all want the same thing
- write it down (maybe not in sexual—it may reduce passion)

- make a plan that you all agree can work at the right pace and a price you can maintain
- Do not keep secrets.
- agree on all aspects of the money.

Not infallible but it's a start. For further advice consult your MP—mayor or congressman—because politics is what they do.

Interviews

Do not on any account be late. Do not think you can blame it on the traffic, your mother, or your horoscope. Put in your mind the appointment time is one hour earlier.

If you arrive early and have to wait, do not play Drunken Dragons on your telephone or iPad; instead find *appropriate* reading. It might be *The Economist*, the FT or WSJ, a trade paper or even a film script. Please NOT *Playboy*, *Captain Marvel* or supermarket tabloids. Why? It is quite likely the one sitting across the desk does this for a living and has developed a few tricks of their own like spying or talking to the receptionist.

Know *exactly* how to get there and where to park. Do a dry run if feasible. If not put on your GPS. Do not ask the man in the streets, who will say "I am from Tristan da Cunha."

If you think you might be late develop measles the day before.

If it so happens you have to rescue a cuddly puppy from a burning building on the way, write—apologizing and saying you understand this disqualifies you and wish him well. You never know.

Answer the question. ONLY the question—fully but briefly.

Try not to answer the wrong question. If you need to adapt to fit your needs, be on your toes. The interviewer knows that one too.

Sometimes a good idea to conclude by repeating the question, particularly if tap-dancing.

Exaggerate a bit if you think it will work, but stick close to the truth. Remember the best lies are just very slight adaptations.

Do not drop a name of any kind.

Even if you happen to be the CEO's favorite child, downplay. "Oh dear! Please don't tell him. He doesn't know I am here!" (You can always sort this out later).

Switch off your telephone.

Do not bring your pet guinea pig even in service animal jacket.

Look up. Do not sink your chin in your chest.

Keep your hands away from your face, which means not biting your nails, picking your nose, taking care of your complexion, or any other domestic hobbies.

Do not tell the examiner/interviewer jokes.

Do not swear, even if he/she does.

Leave the gold Rolex at home even if it is a copy.

During the interview do not use make-up, lipstick or breath freshener.

Dress appropriately (up rather than down), clean your teeth and wash your hair. You are there to make a good impression not show off your jewelry and relevant piercings.

Do not tell him/her the receptionist has nice tits. Do not ask for his/her telephone number.

The same ground rules apply for oral exams:

*When the guy gave me the summons, all I could
do was pay up or offer the bod in lieu. High risk!*

Never mind he actually took me out for a drink afterwards. (**Anonymous actress/film extra**)

Written Exams

A schoolmaster in an Evelyn Waugh novel, wanting quiet, offered the class a cash prize for the longest essay regardless of merit. He had a good idea. Whatever anyone may say papers are often graded on length over scholarship. It may not carry the day but it is a start.

On an English exam no split infinitives or run-on sentences. Eliminate mental tics—e.g. five consecutive sentences beginning with the word *however*—not good.

If you are writing a paper on a book person or play, find some obscure lines or quotations and find a way to shoehorn them in. Yes, you can or you deserve to fail.

If it's math or science you probably have to learn it. If not make sure that with all your calculations you finish with the answer the examiner wants.

There is always the old trick of numbering the pages, omitting the one where you did not know the answer. Unfortunately almost everyone knows that one, so chances of success are slim.

Communicate!

Communication to man's brain is like the knee to his body—essential, but the weakest link.

During the First World War a Colonel in the trenches sent back by word of mouth "Send reinforcements, we're going to advance." The message was duly passed on man by man to HQ. By the time it arrived the message had changed: "Send three and four pence, we're going to a dance."

Whatever you hear on late night television NO ONE is psychic. Unless you are told, you do NOT know, so you guess. It is up to you and everyone else to communicate clearly, understandably, and—preferably—truthfully.

There is plenty of scope for CYA here. All forms of communication can be subject to abuse. Ask the ghost of Richard "Tricky Dickie" Nixon about recording. Funny how unreliable the Ethernet can become when it comes to delivering that email. When it does arrive, how it can be wide open to interpretation.

Face-to-face is good, certainly for matters of hearts or bed.

Ass. U. Me. Don't ever assume, because that is the oldest excuse in the book. "You enjoyed *The Lion King*, so I just assumed you spoke fluent Swahili."

- Plan what you want to communicate.
- Insist on repeating the communication.

- KISS. Too much repetition or fallbacks can lead to irritation, switch off and no reaction.
- Make sure the WHOLE communication is understood.

"I Have to Take This"

No, You Do Not

The telephone was invented unfortunately after Emily Post and Miss Manners had done their best work. Even more unfortunately in our allegedly civilized life it is hard to live without it.

The purpose of the telephone is to communicate. There was a time when you picked it up put your fingers in holes and twisted it. You asked a question, made an appointment or sent good wishes. Then you said goodbye. This was usually someone in your neighborhood. The price was the same as a cup of tea or of those two cigarettes people used to smoke. Not too tricky. Then it was expanded to the "trunk call." The telephone company had an excellent way of regulating this:

(Sfx) "Pip pip pip."

"Oh there go the pips. Must go. Bye."

Happy days, but enough history. Today the telephone has gone mad. The comforting *brrrrr brrrrr* has been replaced by anything from the Hallelujah chorus to AC/DC. What once sat in a corner and looked like a black daffodil has been replaced by something that fits in your pocket and can do anything.

You ring a company (and sometimes an individual) and you are subjected to a series of recordings until eventually you are answered by someone in New Delhi who says her name is Felicity, who speaks limited English, is trying to quiet a screaming baby and says she can help you. Pick the bones out of that.

A few tips about talking on today's telephone:

- Give away as little as possible to an unknown voice. Obvious, but the scammers can be extremely clever.
- Never accept a "free offer." There is no free lunch.
- NO ONE will ever ring you from the tax office. So hang up at once if someone tries that one.
- Remember in public everyone can hear every word you say. Your audience may be fascinated or frustrated. Neither is good.

In many places driving and telephoning can mean a large fine or worse. "It's legal in Mali/Mauritius/Mongolia/Marbella." This will buy you nothing more than a full priced ticket payable within thirty days without the option.

Tempting as it may be, do not get into a pissing contest with a telesales rep. The longer you are on the line the better chance they have to track or scam you.

"You said on the telephone that…" carries as much weight as "I saw on television that…"

On the other hand technology has given us some advantages. Your brain/diary is not clogged up with numbers. In a sticky corner you can have a totally imaginary call. Works very well if you use a headset, because only you know if the telephone has rung at all. The jury is out on headsets. Yes they may look like a deaf aid. They may not go with that expensive hairdo. They may distort your voice; the Bluetooth battery may run low.

On the other hand you can have a private (or an imaginary) conversation. Frees your hands. Easier to deny everything if you get pulled over.

If something important is happening in your life like a drink order, restaurant order, marriage offer, job offer, sex offer, fascinating confession/secret, any gossip, switch the telephone OFF. "I've got to take this…" can kill them all stone-dead. Not a bad form of contraception though, rather like nudity for the over forties.

Some telephone phrases you may hate or like:

"I have to take this." (Today's rudest, most overused sentence.)

"Text that to me."

"You're breaking up."

"I'm only getting one bar."

"My battery is going."

"You must be on an airport runway. All I hear is background noise."

"I must have blocked your number (by mistake)."

"I thought you were a scam."

"You tried to leave a message but my mailbox was full? Oh dear."

E-mails and Texts

Do not put it in an e-mail, do not put it in a text, do not put it on Twitter, do not put it on Facebook UNLESS YOU REALLY MEAN IT AND IT IS THE TRUTH.

Do not text and drive. (See multi-tasking).

Do not propose marriage, breaking up, wild sex, or divorce online.

Do not get involved in politics online. You may know someone of the far left or right (it's usually the far ones) who sends you a diatribe about how Donald Trump eats babies or from this really cool Ghanaian who wants you to join the KKK. DO NOT REPLY. DO NOT FORWARD. DELETE. It is a sure way to lose friends and respect.

Passwords, Personal Security and Privacy

Anyone who thinks privacy exists today has lost the plot. Even when you do decide to take up kale farming in Tierra del Fuego, if someone wants to find you they will.

There are still stories about Arthur who went out to get a bottle of milk and never came back. The truth is that no one cared enough to find him, or he's an integral part of the foundation of the new flyover. Otherwise he'll turn up.

Best advice, unless your ambition is to be on the ten o'clock news, hide in plain sight and try not to do something that will frighten the horses. Make them want to find you.

This does not mean you will not be faced with inventing passwords. Telephones now keep a catalogue of passwords which is fortunate, but rather defeats the purpose. This means, the whole charade is like joining a secret society with a Facebook page.

Best advice: KISS. Include a number - they seem to like that. Do NOT make it short (Some think 'PASSWORD' is a witty password. Its not.) Make it long but memorable to YOU: example (ONLY): 'The quality of Mercy is not stra12neD.' (They often like a capital or two.)

Personal security today is difficult, but then it always was. (Read the first chapter of *A Tale of Two Cities* by Charles Dickens).

If you are obsessive stay out of large crowds and small Italian sports cars, and bore yourself to death instead.

Do not have a couple of drinks and decide it would be fun to explore that ghetto where the police hunt in packs.

NEVER keep your wallet in your back pocket.

NEVER let any credit card out of your sight.

Keep your twenties and above apart from your small change.

Do NOT get advice here about carrying any weapon except mace for women. This is a very personal choice and may well depend on individual circumstances. There are goods and bads on both sides, so think carefully for yourself, and do not listen to a monk in a monastery or prisoner on parole after GBH.

The Invitation to the Ball and Other Social Quicksands

Invited to a party, the Brits bristle with suspicion and a catalogue of reasons to have a bad time: too many people, too few, too much booze, not enough, the bastard/bitch who did/did not hit on me at the last one we forced ourselves to accept. ETCETERA. The high point of the occasion is if someone makes a remark that can be (mis)interpreted to be personally offensive.

The Americans are too busy pricing the furniture or what they call networking to show any enthusiasm. The Scandinavians start well, but may quickly get legless and then maudlin. Oriental hospitality is far too complicated for this slim volume, but it does seem that guests and hosts are always smiling. The Southern Europeans thrive at social occasions for one very good reason: They believe they will enjoy themselves, and therefore do.

To all nationalist groups who have read this far and are starting to dust off their poison pen understand these are generalizations. Having accepted that, see if perhaps there is a grain of truth. To all others who can observe with a wry grin the faults in themselves and their ancestry, just try not to fall into your stereotype.

Being a Guest

- Don't get drunk unless you know exactly what you are doing, which is a contradiction in terms. Well at least try.
- Do not hit on the host's significant other or squeeze for the night, even if it is hard to differentiate one from the other. Either is guaranteed to end in tears.
- Make a point of talking to wallflowers of all colors. They can be far more interesting. The host's stepsister who just inherited a whole chunk of Walmart stock, or be sensational when he/she takes off the glasses or hairpiece. If none of the above, it does make you feel good and look good in the eyes of your host.
- Do not remark on the furnishings unless asked, and even then tread with care. To do so is beyond crass and you may easily say the wrong thing "So you think it's a fake. Hmmm, interesting the man from Sothebys begs to differ" or "You like that? You must be drunk! Alastair's second wife gave it to him." (*Hot salt tears ensue*).
- Do not have a knockdown drag out with your significant other for any reason. It could be accidental, but just as likely terminal. Save it for the journey home. You never know it may end in make-up sex.
- Leave before either the host or hostess goes to bed.
- On an upmarket overnight stay leave a little something for the maid. Do not do this if you are sleeping on the pullout bed of your college roommate, who you know might (or might not) be changing the sheets him/herself.
- In a private house do not open any cupboard, borrow the telephone or use the computer. All are bad man-

ners, and anyway you may uncover something you wish you had not.

- In a private club do not tip the staff. Only exception: a surreptitious piece of folding to the table waiter at a company function to keep the wine or liquor flowing.
- Always always say thank you. Not just a drunken slap on the back as you leave, but the box of Bendix Bittermints, the Widow Clicquot, the bunch of roses still aglow with the morning dew. Well if it was not that great an evening scale it down, but do it.

Personal Security

- Gatecrashing. This is like adolescence. It is something we all go through, and like adolescence we never quite grow out of it. If you really feel you have to be there, have an entry strategy as well as an exit one. PLEASE do not try the "invitation lost in the post" that has whiskers on it and could lose you all kinds of points even if you get to stay. "You must not have my new address" is a little better, but not much. Better try: "Your sister Jemima insisted I came. Against all my principles I have to say, but I have even brought you some (*fill in the blank*) as a peace offering." That should do the trick, unless last time you met you suggested a secret runaway weekend in Paris and did not or did make good on your promise.

Being a Host

- Beware of gatecrashers. They can very very rarely make the evening. More likely ruin it. The world's best gatecrasher is said to be Bill Murray. He is known to walk into a party unannounced, saying nothing, empty the ashtrays, wash some glasses, hand around a plate of canapés, and leave. He is of course Bill Murray.

- Do NOT try and get John and Mary back together just because the decree is still Nisi and you think they belong together. They know better than you do.
- Do not try and hit your guests up for money. If they agreed to pay five hundred for the tickets or the blind auction, settle it before or after the occasion (better before).
- RIK stands for Row In Kitchen. Do not have one.
- If you value it hide it or put it in the bank. As Alan Bennett once said "Victoria has been sick on the Aubusson." And she will again. If someone spills red wine on the white carpet, it was quite likely an accident (if not God was probably watching and you had it coming). So do not spend the next hour with a damp rag, a container of salt, white wine or other fave cleaner. Cover it with a rug from your bedroom and move on.
- Lock your bedroom door. You may ask why. Don't argue. Just do it.
- Do not overpromise anything. Just because you sent Lady Gaga an invitation does not mean she will show.
- Many will disagree with this: Do not give a party on a boat. It's a lovely idea, drifting down the river in the sunset of a summer's day with the romantic aroma of diesel fumes, and Victoria being sick on the canapés this time. You can only go home when the boat docks, not when you decide.

Leaving Pub or Party

Try not to be the last to leave. If his/her answer all evening has been NO, it is unlikely it will change with last orders or the last waltz.

After the pub closes is the time when most scraps start, and you may get drawn into one that is not yours. This may well lead to the arrival of Lily Law, who are known to hang around at that time waiting for an easy score, which is boring even if you are not driving.

At a party be sure to leave before the host goes to bed, or falls asleep on the sofa. Try to remember not to get into the bath and spend the night there. There are many examples of both. Really.

The best way to leave either pub or party is NOT to smother the host with loud insincere thanks. Sending flowers if relevant is much more effective. Better solution is to separate from the herd, look slightly abstracted, NOT speak, open the door and move out of sight asap.

And Oh, the People You'll Meet!

Friends

Not everyone you meet is going to be your best friend, but it's not a bad starting point.

Think of friendship as a pyramid, but made of LEGO, because you can and will change the bricks at any time. You may need or want to change the shape a bit or perhaps the colors are wrong.

This pyramid is layered:

1. The significant other. The pointy bit at the top. If that is not true, remove. Replace with care.
2. Immediate family. This level is optional, but with any luck it is there. Your parents and siblings almost certainly know more about you than anyone.
3. Next come your mates/BFF's or buddies. The weakest and the strongest part of the pyramid. Weakest because they are the easiest to misidentify; strongest because if you have it right they can be the most solid.
4. Those with shared important experience hardship or even extreme joy create an unbreakable bond. They may rise to be part of no. 3 above. Not necessarily.

5. Work and social acquaintances. They may become part of nos. 3 or 4 above. Or not.
6. The rest of the world. Some may be clamoring for inclusion, some for exclusion.

The big difference between the pyramid of friendship and the Egyptian original is that friendship needs constant maintenance. Friends have shortcomings. For example their own lives, moving, friends of their own (whose company they prefer to yours), death. For these and many other reasons your friends change. Sad, but inevitable. Do not force the issue. When it becomes obvious—move on. In friendship as in marriage.

Although it sometimes seems doubtful the truth is they are human; therefore they have faults. Just like you. So judge on compatibility not quality. If you cannot accept the faults of a friend you do not have a friend. And may never.

A lot of rubbish is talked about cross-gender friendship. Of course it is possible, but you should sort out the sexual thing first. That does not *necessarily* mean consummation, but it does mean having an understanding, albeit tacit. Dealing with that later can cause all kinds of problems. *When Harry met Sally* included the greatest (non)sex scene of all time, but was not the only piece of fiction.

Many brag they can be friends with anyone. True but flawed thinking because it may well confuse nos. 3, 4 and even 5. The number of no. 4 category friends is most likely to being in direct contrast to no. 3.

Human nature being what it is, nearly all gravitate toward their social and racial equals. Thus there are cricket clubs in Los Angeles and Americans have softball teams in London. During World War II even the French in London managed to get along for the sake of La Patrie.

Today black may marry white and king may marry commoner and this is hopefully a sign perhaps the old way is breaking down. Human nature may beg to differ, for prejudice is a hardy oft nurtured growth.

Straight or Gay

Enough has been written on this tortured and now unfortunately mangled subject.

Good or bad, innate or learned, important or trivial, gay exists. Always has, always will. Human society is infinitely enriched by its gay members. Fortunately it is no longer taboo or the subject for sniggering by adolescents of all ages. Unfortunately it is still the subject of prejudice and the barbarian sport of "queer bashing" is still far too prevalent.

Golfers join golf clubs, gamblers go to casinos, singers join choirs. Gay people go to gay bars or clubs, where so-called "straight people" may well feel out of place. Then again unless it is your thing, do you really want to spend an evening discussing golf club handle grips, or whether to play Texas hold 'em or Seven-card stud?

Its worst facet is when straight or gay is forced into the public eye. Do not preach. Do not flaunt (see Making Out in Public.) Do not discuss (see Religion). Hetero or homo, sex or friendship, do it, enjoy it and do not bore everyone else with it (see Sport).

Ship's Bore

In days of yore P&O, Cunard and Thomas Cook were in charge of Abroad and P.O.S.H meant something (Port Out, Starboard Home).

Even then seasoned travelers had an unbreakable rule: Do not befriend the first person to whom you speak; he is bound to be the ship's bore.

This rule still applies, if with variance. Cruises are a holiday popular with many. BEWARE! He (usually) knows a thing or two about "life on the briny," and will latch like a limpet as you find your cabin or standing awkward during lifeboat drill. This means meeting in the bar for a little drinkie, while he has a word with a pal so he can be at your dining table for "fun-packed days afloat."

The rule can be applied any time groups of strangers are assembled—tours, hotels, school, university, conscription, conventions, prison, airport delays…geddit?

One film technician bedded a make-up girl on the first day of a location feature film and found himself to be half "an item" for the next twelve weeks. His mates were in different bars, brothels and beds every night as he was fighting off invitations to meet Mom.

It's all in the timing.

Experts

"Experts" are everywhere. From the cab driver who knows the city like the back of his hand to the car mechanic who is factory trained (it was a frozen food factory), to the IT guy who can fix your computer forever (once he finds the off/on switch), to the financial adviser whose best recommendation is a dead cert 100–1 chance for the Derby.

There are indeed experts who do know a thing or two, but go with useless until proven effective.

Perhaps the worst kind of experts are the telephone helplines that take you direct to a center by the Ganges.

If you need an expert get a reference of some kind, particularly if the expertise is coming free. It is very often better to pay (and get a receipt). Then at least you have some redress.

The most unreliable of all call themselves "financial consultants." On his website it says "Left the brokerage house of ffitch, ffrench and Fitch because he felt his very clear insight into the markets was of outstanding value…"

CAN'T WE ALL GET ALONG?

First Impression

Let no one tell you anything different. First impressions are important. Best advice: Start vanilla, and then keep your wits about you. Remember pacemakers often finish last, so let others take the lead.

Good first impressions include the following:

- small smile - NOT great Pepsodent number
- tempered Enthusiasm - NOT backslapping "You and and I going to be real mates/BFF."
- knowledge or appreciation - NOT "Could you sign my T-shirt under the arm?"
- sensible handshake: NOT finger cracker or wet fish
- something interesting to say: not your life story.
- accepted greeting of the nation: Handshake for the French Cheek kiss for Hispanics; nose rub for Inuits? You decide
- Go with the flow. If you do well first time, you will not lose points if you (with skill, tact, and charm) say what you really think as things develop.

Bad First Impressions include

- Being Late
- Mumbling and being shy
- Looking at your feet.
- Not talking
- Looking over the shoulder.
- Being Late
- "I have to take this"
- Being Drunk,
- Public personal hygiene, lack of or fixing.
- Jokes (good, bad. lavatory),
- Being late
- Hitting the dog, the cat or the parrot.
- Hitting on the parent.
- Humblebrag
- Flashing the Gold Rolex
- Being late.

Temper

Bad Temper

Losing it is about as bad an idea as it gets. You lose control, respect, time, energy and a great deal else. It is a bit like being drunk and has the same result for you and others.

If you do go apeshit—and we all do it at some time—admit it *once* and turn it into a joke against yourself. Try not to revisit.

Pretending to lose it sometimes works, but be very careful. It can have very bad blowback.

Having a reputation for bad temper may strike fear in some, but never respect.

Good Temper

It would be nice to say always be good tempered, but that too has its problems. You may seem to be a buffoon or a soft touch.

Surprise!

Always fun to surprise someone, isn't it! NOT always!

A wife thought it would be fun to surprise her husband by meeting him at the airport. He came through the door of mystery with his arms around someone else. Yes it was certainly a surprise, but only the lawyers really enjoyed it.

Surprise visits are not a good idea unless you know the surprise very well. Even then you may well arrive at the wrong time, in the middle of a row/divorce or make-up sex.

Choose surprise gifts with great care. Stay away from cute little kittens and puppies; they don't stay cute and little for long and may turn into unwanted liabilities. Even if *you* do, not everyone adores hamsters, guinea pigs or pythons. You will be fine to give chocolates, Cutty Sark or champagne as long as they fit the lifestyle and diet. Tickets to the Electric Wallpaper Farewell tour can also work, but not just because you once met the bass guitarist and it's your favorite band. Expensive jewelry almost always works, but it may be more than you can afford and more commitment than you had in mind.

Surprises might be fun or might be a disaster.

> *Open your mouth and close your eyes and you*
> *might catch some great big flies.* (**ANON**)

Jokes

Best advice: Don't tell jokes. You may think they are funny; others may find them weak, tasteless or incomprehensible. The only possible reason to tell one is because they are completely relevant to the moment. If you feel you must, tell it if possible as a true story.

Having said that you will probably be tempted. We all are. In that case remember the following:

- Always laugh at other people's jokes because that is a great way to make friends.
- Lavatory, racial or sexist jokes—it is astonishing how easy it is to lose friends this way, so think twice or forget the punch line.
- Never try and top another joke. You are highly unlikely to top the first laugh and you are quite likely to piss someone off.
- Never, never, never tell an actor a joke. An actor is inclined not to work every day so he hangs around in bars, and he has probably heard that one. An actor's job is acting, so he will tell it better than you.
- If you must tell a joke keep it as short as possible, unless of course you ARE an actor.

Thank You

Not difficult, but not quite as easy as it looks. Effusive does not cover for sincere, and genuine appreciation trumps both. A casual almost thrown away mention of the usefulness of the gift/gesture and advice in later conversation does a lot more than hugs and air-kissing at the time.

For hospitality and money always WRITE thank you. Be brief if you like as long as you mean it even if you don't.

Flowers or chocolates can work a treat.

Swearing

Be very careful. VERY careful. It is okay if you are with the guys in the bar, and you have known each other since kindergarten. Otherwise don't, particularly if you are a girl. Some people swear because they think it's macho. Others swear because it might be a bonding thing. In that case look very carefully at the bond.

There was once a young ambitious marketing executive who was fired because he told his very senior client he had done some f— —ing good advertising for him. (Turned out the client was an elder in a "Wee Free" Scottish church).

It has been said that he with the potty mouth has some real or imagined inadequacies…worth thinking about.

> *It's not funny and it's not clever, so stop it.*
> (**Anonymous Victorian nanny**)

Social Blunders

Anyone who says they have never put their foot in it has led a very sheltered and boring life, or more likely is telling a whopper (see Lying). The vast majority of us have a collection of blush making, wake-in-the-middle-of-the-night horror stories.

You say you will never do something that stupid again. You will. Such is life.

Take heart on two accounts. Everyone worth knowing has done it. It may seem important to you, but there is a *very* good chance the one into whose mouth you put your foot, has forgotten or forgiven. If not it is someone you never need to see again or want to keep on your speed dial.

Best advice—no *only* advice: Apologize once and MOVE ON. Everyone worthwhile will.

Desperation: Go to confession. Failing that it is the pistol in the darkened room. (Better not to leave a confess-all note. But you will, because everyone always does.)

Advice

The chances of your advice being taken are slim to none. If it is, you and only you may well be held responsible for the dog/hamster/python, the marriage, the divorce, the career, or the microbrewery Real Ale.

> *Advice is wonderful, blame is its ugly stepsister.*
> (**Marjorie Proops, 60s Agony Aunt**) attrib

Lying

There was an English prime minister who would look into the very large television camera of his day and say "Quite honestly…" and you knew there was a whopper coming. He is reputed to have had a taste for Cuban cigars and had a government employee who stood by the front door of Number 10 holding a Gannex coat and a pipe, waiting for him to appear before the press and public. There was an American president who "Did not inhale" and Sadly the more powerful you are the bigger lies you can—and will—tell.

Never, never, never, ever trust anyone who says: "I always tell the truth," because that is a lie.

Sad to say we all tell them from time to time. Sometimes to flatter, sometimes to get something (okay…someone perhaps) you MUST have, sometimes to get out of trouble, sometimes to save or make money. None are very honorable, but all are universal.

We are not hearing confession, so relax. You know what you said, so blush and move on. Just stick as close to the truth as possible.

One heartfelt request: Do not tell a whopper to get someone into trouble; you will feel badly if you do. You will be found out, and you will lose both respect and friends.

A tip: You find the suspect of the amazing story about saving dear little kiddies from an ice floe on the River Seine and being shortlisted for the Croix de Guerre which meant not getting to the bank and needing a thousand Krone (in cash please if that's okay): Ho Ha Hum. Just ask for the story to be repeated backwards.

Cheating at solitaire or patience is lying to yourself. (**The Hon Guy Strutt**)

Apologies

A lot like thanks. Do it once—with gift if you must. Mean it. Move on.

Do NOT mention it every time you meet.

Flattery

Do not be misled. Flattery is a powerful and irresistible drug; it can get you anywhere.

A word of warning: Anyone who is worth of flattering is likely to be smart enough to see through flannel, although self-admiration may still color judgement. Misplaced or misconstrued it can leave the flatterer with a lot of egg on the face and no exit strategy.

Thus flattery should be used with care and thought.

Festina Lente

An old bull and a young bull are standing on the far side of the field when the farmer lets in a herd of cows.

The young bull says: "Look at that! Let's charge down and screw a couple of them!"

The old bull says: "No. We'll walk down and screw all of them."

For a variety of reasons speed is too often considered to be essential. Thus people take in half the communication (to impress?), cut corners (laziness?), take the shortcut they do not understand (trying to impress?), leave the top of the toothpaste, scotch, and ant farm (who cares?).

There are a thousand clichés in the haste makes waste category. Sad to say, they are all true.

Enthusiasm

Genuine enthusiasm is the spice of life. The English are usually very bad at it.

Know When to Raise the White Flag

No one is always right, whatever you or they may think. So if surrounded by crocodiles with loud voices and victory seems impossible, leave, shrug like a French person or even agree.

You may lose the battle, but you may well win the war.

What Robert "the Bruce" really said to the spider that time in the cave: "If you don't succeed at first—give up." (**Anthony Shaffer**).

"If Only…"

The stupidest game of all. Some people try it as a cure for insomnia. All that does is make you frustrated, and you only fall asleep ten minutes before the alarm.

You did not/could not/had not, and probably will not. So get over it and move on.

Don't sweat the small stuff, and it's all small stuff. (**Feel-good American psychotherapy cliché**)

Never Sell Your Soul to Man

There is a belief that hookers are the only ones that sell their bodies.

That may indeed seem true, but there are other more subtle, more invidious, longer lasting forms of flesh peddling.

There are two kinds of stars, whether they be film, sports, music, business or just in their own lunchtime:

Either

"This is amazing! Here I am with more money than my dear old dad made in his lifetime. How long will it last? Time to save!"

Or

"This is amazing! Here I am with more money than my dear old dad made in his lifetime. How long will it last? Time to SPEND!"

FACT—the number of lottery winners who go broke is exceeded only by the number of Sports Stars who spend through contracts worth more than the GDP of a not-so-small country.

Of course this second group cannot do it on their own. Car dealers and property developers do their best, but their real helpers are their friends and relations. Nice work if you can get it? You may clean the shoes, take out the rubbish, run to the bar to order drinks, stay up all night, take the blame and stand bail for the "misunderstandings" or breathe into the bag or provide the sample after a heavy night.

That is just the good side. What is worse is you have sold yourself into slavery. You may not be pickin' that cotton, bailin' that hay; what you have may be more comfortable, but is just as demanding all for a little reflected glory and some name dropping and photo ops.

Never Sell Your Soul to Corporate

Of course *you* would never do that.

However you had to cancel that cruise because there was that big presentation. And then you had to cover for Monica who was on maternity leave. Pity about those days between Christmas and New Year's Day, but someone had to take care of things. Why did Aunt Bess organize the family reunion at your busiest time of the year? You fill in the blanks.

Three things wrong with THAT life:

1. You become the one who can be relied on to take up the slack. But that must be good! Wrong. You are viewed as the one who has no ties outside the office; you are used until your best-by date. You are then of no further use. It is sadly NOT the way promotion lies.

2. Things will change—that is life's one constant. The manager who referred to you as "good old reliable" gets promoted overseas, gets incurable chilblains or gets fired. Suddenly you are dead wood that needs trimming, or worse still you find a permanent place in the file marked middle aged, middle class, middle management.

3. You have missed out on your own life, and you only get one of those. No one is going to remember you worked five weekends in a row, and there will be a line of people there to take the credit for you.

Best Advice: Don't trust the hand that feeds, although there is no need to bite it. Both happen, so better not to take the feed.

Never Sell Your Soul to In-Laws

Marriage sets in motion wheels you never imagine.

It is very easy to be sucked into the family of your spouse. It may start with going for lunch on Sunday. This morphs into a Christmas pony for that niece with the runny nose and pigtails, who used your computer without asking and wiped all your emails. Then you have to find a job for Gerry who just finished three years for GBH but really is going straight this time.

Best advice: Do NOT buy that really nice three up three down you cannot really afford that just happens to be on the same street as the couple you now refer to as Mom and Dad.

You married the one you love, not her family. There is a school of thought that says an appreciable number of marriage breakdowns start with the in-laws.

If you choke down the piece of fruit cake you hate and say "How delicious!" you will be treated with it on every visit. If you fix the gutter on the roof you may well be labeled as a great pair of hands and summoned for anything from changing a light bulb to a major automotive overhaul, because "who needs to pay a so-called mechanic!"

There really is no free lunch, and with the feeding hand a sense of ownership develops, sometimes intentional, sometimes not.

> *You may not like marriage, but it is the only game in town.* (**Seth Holt - oft married film director**)

Measure Twice Cut Once

Even if you were once voted "The one most likely to make it as a carpenter or a tailor" still do it.

In sex, love and marriage measure everything and measure at least twice.

In life as in cloth or wood, *Check your work*—whoever you are, whatever it is, even in less important things like life choices and careers.

Opportunity Knocks

When that unexpected offer comes out of nowhere certainly measure twice, but do it quickly and positively.

No you do not need to drive the getaway car for a badly organized bank robbery with the cousin of the Barmaid.

Yes you do want to take the three-week all expenses gig in Barbados with that dreamboat you just met, even if it means postponing/canceling legover with Tracy or Jason whose parents have taken the caravan to the seaside for the weekend.

If possible go for it, but you may need to massage the facts explaining to others because you will have to live with consequences.

> *I have had a subsequent offer from richer and more influential friends.* (**End of a beautiful friendship**)

Always Volunteer

How often have you heard "What! Me? Volunteer? You have got to be kidding." Dumb—very dumb. Why? If you volunteer odds on it's going to be a special gig—more interesting. You will not have to do what the rest are doing. You are already one step ahead.

If it's in your job, you will as like as not meet the higher ups and as equals. You have established your identity. The bad news? The doofus at the next desk, who went out for a smoke when he heard they wanted volunteers, will be jealous. Tsk. Tsk.

Socially all of the above apply. Moreover you will look like a hero… Who knows who?

Gossip

Listen. You might hear something interesting.

Do not start and do not repeat. If you cannot resist, double check your source(s) before calling the TV news.

Do not be the subject. Easier said than done, but possible. If you are, defuse it by confronting. The truth is good but may need a little massage. (Keep that to a minimum).

Keep your own counsel, but listen to the BS of others.

> *Speak softly and carry a big stick; you will go far.* (**Theodore Roosevelt**)attrib.

Never Argue Politics or Religion

In vino (semi) veritas we all do it. Do not expect any love to come from it. You will convert no one, possibly lose friends and may come out with a bad rep as being more extreme than you are.

If you find yourself being drawn in, take evasive action. Leave, study the test card on the television, start reading War and Peace in, and put the hit on someone's squeeze. If asked for an opinion say: "Do you know the one about the bishop, the rabbi and Ousama Ben Laden, who all go into a brothel?"

The advice to avoid is acknowledged and too often ignored.

Poor Me

You look with envy at Mr. and Ms. Teflon over there, whose life goes ever upwards without upset. Highly unlikely; they are either in major cover-up mode, or up for the Nobel Prize for boredom.

More likely no one shares the crises of Maison Teflon because no one there ever says: "Life is just not FAIR!"

If you have not noticed the unfairness of life, you have not been paying attention.

If you feel sorry for yourself, you do not need—nor will you get any help from anyone else.

Name-Dropping Etc.

It is not good to claim or even infer the confidence of a star in your firmament and refer to him as "Bob" when everyone who really knows him knows he hates that and is known as RJ.

A lowly film technician became a crew joke because say he said he was lunching with the star, only to be seen alone in the pub with a stale ham sandwich.

Name dropping. You will do it. We all do it; it gives us a buzz and impresses our adoring public.

Underplay the name drop. Far more impressive when the subject of your drop buys you a drink than your cow-eyes following him to the gents.

> *Oh I really wish Sly Stallone would stop inviting me out for drinks. He always insists on paying the bill.* (**Humblebrag**—YUCK)

Foreign Languages

Unless you are absolutely fluent and have an impeccable accent, do not speak French to Parisians. They will despise you even more (yes just possible) and adjust the price accordingly.

With the Italians smile broadly, and wave your arms about a lot. They want to understand you, and you will enjoy the whole deal.

The Spanish speaking from Spain or the Americas go all the way to understand with words gestures and warm embraces.

It is worth noting there are now three languages in the United States: English, Spanish and Spanglish, which is used almost as much as the other two.

With Scandinavians there is no problem. They learnt English at school, are very well mannered and speak English as well as you do except when drunk and/or suicidal, both of which happen.

The Germans are the same if less polite; they attribute their language skills to overlong military occupation.

Holland is like a part of the United Kingdom. The Dutch are warmer and often more fun than the English and even play cricket quite well.

If you and one other in a group are fluent in another language, speaking it is guaranteed to annoy. It looks as if you are talking about everyone else. (You may well be—just save it for later.)

Criticism

Do not criticize a man's dog, wife, relations, or TV picture. He himself may not like any one of them, but they are his, and he has to live with them, so your opinion is NOT welcome.

Q Barging – aka Line Management

This is an acquired skill. The most expert are the French because standing in line is an anathema to them; it reminds them of those Napoleon called a nation of shopkeepers namely the English.

The least skilled are the Spanish who are polite, really don't care and can always find someone to chat with unless the queue is for the bathroom.

Move with care. Nothing is more embarrassing than a loud high-pitched eight-year-old voice that says "Daddy, why is that person pushing in front of us?" except perhaps "No you go ahead. You're obviously in a hurry. I'll find the disabled line."

The trick is to move only when the whole queue is moving. Adopt a faraway, slightly worried and sad look and avoid the eyes of others.

In defending against others a carefully placed foot can cause just the right amount of disruption. If you yourself are tripped try "No it's fine. You were not to know it was the leg that got shot up in Dunkirk, Korea, Vietnam, Iraq etc. etc."

Getting There Is Less Than Half the Fun!

FLYING

In one word—DON'T.

In seven words—NEVER fly with or near small children.

Trouble is that it is easier said than done. There are those who do not or will not, but that makes life very limiting. So become a hermit or bite the bullet. Just remember it is unlikely to be fun.

You may think what follows is common sense. It is. However ALL the advice is based on incidents that have appeared on the (international) news, or can be guaranteed to have happened, most to seasoned travelers.

Paying

Never ever pay cash for a ticket. It sets off alarm bells with security, and you can be almost certain you will be stopped on suspicion of being the ghost of Ousama Ben Laden. Very embarrassing.

Packing

- Take as little as possible. If you are going for more than three days and less than three weeks you are more than likely to come across a washer drier (Europe, Australia, US etc.) or elsewhere someone delighted to do washing for a lot less than the cost of overweight.
- Do not take that smart Louis Vuitton suitcase. It may look great as you wait for your chauffeur-driven limousine outside the five-star hotel (where you are probably NOT staying.) That's what an unseen airline/airport employee might think too.
- Ninety-nine percent of Airline people are pure as the driven snow and live with their mom and dad and sponsor the cats home and the children's home, etc. The other 1 percent can do all the damage necessary; so if you value it, do not pack it.
- Make sure you do not have your special Swiss Army knife in your pocket, or the derringer strapped to your ankle, or anything else. You will lose it for absolute certain even if you are wearing your nun's habit, an all over plaster of Paris body cast or your collar back to front.
- You will be better treated if you dress up rather than down.
- You may think those white stretchy socks are a bit sissy. Just remember they save lives.
- Do NOT wear tight shoes. Your feet swell at 30000 ft.
- Do not agree to buy, send or bring anything. It will waste your time, and the chance of seeing the money are on a par with being handcuffed to a ghost.
- Never ever agree to take with you anything anywhere for anyone unless you know them well. NOT the blonde

you met in the bar who promised you wild sex on your next trip; NOT the ex-pat with the funny teeth; NOT even the business colleague who wants you to take his mom's birthday present.

At the Airport

- Arrive early—no, arrive very early.
- Anyone, however rich, who parks their car at the airport needs professional help unless he "knows a guy," can do the expenses/tax trick, or is coming back VERY soon.
- A less well-known fact. Anyone can get a wheelchair. If you have something more serious than a hangnail it can be a very good idea. It gets you early boarding. It gets you the sympathy vote. If you play it right it may even get you into one of those business class clubs where you are often treated like a human being. Perhaps most important the wheelchair can save a lot of wear and tear on the bod. For example changing planes at Frankfurt can mean a mile walk. German travelers tend to be very fit, but not your best friends.
- Make sure you have photo ID, the flight number, and something to read. Make sure your computer, telephone, watch etc. are fully charged. All simple stuff you say. You know all that. Oh really? Good.
- Look at the official airport signs. The airport wants you out asap, to make room for the next sucker, so the signage is usually pretty good.
- Before you relax get within reach of your gate, make sure it is the right one. You know all that? Oh really? Good.

- If you think there is a shadow of a glimmer of a chance, ask for an upgrade. You just never know. You will find this works much better if you exude confidence and have dressed up, not down.
- Sympathy in the air travel industry is in short supply. Dressing like a Goodwill poster child with a hangdog expression will do nothing but send you to the back of the line.
- Do NOT mess with security. They have had the humor gene surgically removed.
- If you have it, they will find it, and you will NOT get it back.
- Best plan for going through security is to empty your pockets and put it ALL in your bag/carry-on—including your headset.
- Do NOT get drunk at the airport bar. A beer/scotch is fine, but there is no mileage in more. The booze is very expensive, and if you talk to the guy on the next stool you may find yourself knowing more about diets of rodents than you ever wanted—oh yes and paying for his drinks.
- Pay for one drink at a time—yours.

Remember: if you board the plane falling about you will lose the friendship of the cabin crew and your fellow passengers. If you are really out of hand you might add the pilot to that list, and that is serious.

Duty Free

Time was when anyone going to Canada, Colombia, Cadiz or Calais was honor bound to bring back a bottle of Scotch and 200 extra strong untipped cigarettes in a red tin. Today not so much. Few smoke, and you can probably score a bottle of scotch at your local Superstore cheaper than the bottle of 50 year old single malt, which happens to be the only one the Duty Free shop has in stock.

If you see a piece of electronics or a gadget without which you cannot live, have at it. However just remember, even if you do not get stopped arriving home, if you take it out of the country you can get nicked then. Just saying.

If you like certain white powders NOT prescribed by the doctor, or even herbal cigarettes—well good luck with that. You may be lucky, but if you are not, well it can change your life. Just ask Stacey Keach and others.

If you go East - don't…don't…don't touch any of that stuff. Midnight Express was the General Admission certificate movie of what might happen to you.

Never lose sight of your own stuff, and do NOT agree to mind that of anyone else. When that dear little old lady asks you to put her badly wrapped package on your trolley going through customs the answer is a resounding NO. Customs BTW know one more joke than security—you.

Thirty Thousand Feet

Once you get on the aircraft, airlines have you by the short hairs. Do not fight it, because you will lose; the only question is how badly.

If you turn left when you arrive at the plane a lot of what follows is less relevant, but not all of it. So read on.

- Avoid the middle seats. Aisle is best.
- Avoid children.
- Try for the emergency door row.
- Do not beat time with your foot on the seat in front.

- Do not ask the cabin staff for their telephone number.
- Do not refer to any one of them as a flying waitress—particularly the male ones. They have heard that one often, and they did not think it was funny the first time.
- Do not try and sit in the wrong seat because you think you might be on a promise with the blonde in row 17. You will be moved, and you will not make friends.
- Do not think you will finish that report you meant to do last night. Do what you like: set out all your notes and your laptop, polish your glasses, put on your best Apprentice look. Not impressed. Within half an hour you will be playing Spider or watching a soppy movie.
- Most important: get up and walk around. Your bod will be most grateful. Get a glass of orange juice, water, anything. You can try and chat to the cabin crew. (Do not expect anything more than a polite reply and paste on smile; they are on break. Very few of them date the public, whatever soft porn fantasies you may have).

Arrivals

- Do not stand up until the aircraft comes to a stop. It does not get you out any faster. No one will be amused when you reach up to get your carry-on, and it rips the neatly folded cashmere coat next to it, or lands on the head of the dear sweet little old lady whose son just happens to be a lawyer.
- Make sure the suitcase you take off the carousel is yours. A lot of bags look the same and try putting it right from your hotel.
- Odds are the arrival temperature will be different from the departure.

- Have a plan to escape from the airport. Cab, Uber, train, bus, Mom, best friend, secret love assignation—all good. Man with big smile you have never seen before, who knows the city promises a large black limousine—not good.
- When you have checked out of your hotel, spent your last money, maxed out your credit cards, and the biweekly flight has been cancelled—all bets are off, and the Consul has gone home.

All these suggested mishaps happen to all air travelers—even the most seasoned, and that is an average to good trip.

All we can offer are two platitudes:

- Time to spare? Go by air.
- Hope for the best, and prepare for the worst. Alternative: Don't Fly.

CAR: PURCHASE

- Always remember Car Dealers are the direct descendants of the Horse Traders of yore, with all the same tricks of the trade. The only difference: it was easier to see if a horse was lame.
- You may think you are the great negotiator. Beware - the harder they trade the harder you fall.
- Every dealer has a price below which they will not go. This figure has nothing to do with the sticker price; the problem is getting there.
- Do not be fooled by: "I have had three other offers on this little beauty. Now I am a man of my word, but

unfortunately my boss says I can only give you until the end of the day." *Uh Huh.*

- Do not be fooled by: "This is the car I would buy myself."
- Do not be fooled by: "I wish you could have met the sweet little old lady who only brought it in because it was too much horsepower."
- Try as hard as possible to buy new, even if you really had your heart set on the one with the fish tail dual exhaust, the go faster stripes and the studio quality sound system.
- If you cannot do that, find an old banger you can run into the ground, but before you buy it get someone who knows an inlet manifold from a Playboy Centerfold to have a look.
- Try to avoid buying on payments. Do you really want to pay an extra 33% to someone you have never met?
- Once you make the commitment, when you go to trade it in, and you will, the new wheels for which you had to give up taking Sandra from Accounts Payable to the pub, will have the value to buy you another new set. Geddit?
- Resign yourself to losing the arm-wrestle with the salesman. Just try and make it as painless as possible.
- Almost without exception a flash car is for a flash Harry. Not always true, certainly not of the suddenly rich, but high profile people are inclined to buy low profile cars.
- Buy an SUV. If you are so posh you never need the motor for a trip to the rubbish dump or taking home six short planks and ten gallons of green paint from the local DIY, you can take it next time you go to watch

Polo and let out two well-bred Golden Retrievers with feathery tails or Salukis with diamond collars.

- Do not feel badly about that good looking blond stud in the Porsche, who beat you to the draw on your favourite barista. If she prefers that kind of flash to your wit and charm she was probably not worth the bother anyway. As for him, tell yourself ten years from now what hair he has left will be grey, and he will be parking a beige banger outside The Purple Pussy Cat, where he works.

Aftercare

Buying the car is just the first step. Your new best friend from now on is your service tech. Treat this relationship with as much care as a marriage. Like an unhappy spouse, he can break you in every sense. You may find true love first time around; if not move on.

Do what he says. Changing oil, battery, or gear box is an expensive, time-consuming bore. Would you rather be sitting in the stuffy, fume-filled cab of the tow truck that kept you waiting for two hours and charges cash only, by the mile *and* the minute.

Brakes and tires—check and maintain—or perhaps you would rather be sitting in the stuffy…etc. etc.

Car sticker price means a lot less than car care, and that means not ignoring flashing lights AND not keeping the pizza box, dirty socks etc. inside the car, or the dead flies on the front. If someone writes in the grime "This car needs washing" it does not always come out with the first or even second wash.

Buy and keep the really good insurance, because on all roads you are surrounded by assassins.

Do not jump out of your car and brag how good your insurance is. You may find that being tested.

It costs a lot more to knock a dent out of a Bentley than a banger. Insurance companies know that too, so read the fine print before you sign for the cut rate. If you have or know an insurance broker buy him a drink. Cheaper than buying the front end of a Ferrari.

Think carefully before you get a personalized number plate. Looks fun and flash, but it makes you very noticeable by friends and cops alike. "I saw you parked outside The Purple Pussycat. I thought you said you were spending the night in silent prayer." Hard to deny if you have a plate that says "SHAGHIWAY."

Unless you take up long distance truck driving for profit and pleasure you do not really spend that much time with your wheels, so do not spend too much.

Road Rage

Do you really want to spend the night as a guest of Her Maj or Tom Selleck and his NY Blue Bloods just because some dingbat in a rice burner with go-faster stripes takes the bit of road you had your eye on?

DOGS, CATS, FISH, HUMANS AND OTHER PETS

Animals as pets are great. They alleviate loneliness, do not answer back, do not hate your hairstyle, or mind you were stinking drunk last night.

Dogs treated well will think you are perfect, and we all need someone like that in our life.

Cats know they are superior beings and are not fooled. Like any significant other they require you to work at the relationship; your reward is equal to your contribution, but worth every moment.

A word of warning: Not everyone may share your affection for little Poochie-Woochie. Therefore do NOT take P-W uninvited to a party, interview, date, religious service, significant other's family reunion, office picnic, restaurant (particularly Chinese where his brother might be on the menu).

"I'm going to bring Poochie-Woochie with me. He is no trouble!"

The length of pause before reply is the best way to judge the reaction.

If P-W bites the host or pees on the Aubusson, look for new friends. If you laugh, look forward to a life of celibacy, or leave town in the morning.

You may find dogs used in the dating game:

"Listen Poochie-Woochie! It's Daddy on the phone!" "Funny how he likes his head on the pillow." "He's usually snoring by the sports news." "When he makes that noise he really needs walkies! Do you mind?"

Be it threat or warning - it is decision time.

Cats are smarter. They make nice with the one person who hates all animals. If no lap is on offer, there is the nice soft cashmere or the football fan shirt, flung off perhaps in reckless passion.

Cats are totally opinionated judges of the likelihood and suitability of proposed nookie. You may try bribery and shows of affection, but these do not guarantee success. Do not complain if you wake up with a stiff neck and your chin welded to your sternum; it is your punishment for daring to share his pillow.

Fish are less sociable and swims quietly up and down past the treasure chest and the man in the old-fashioned diving gear, causing no emotional tug on the heartstrings; they are prone to all kinds of disease and rarely react well to an aspirin or vaccination. Cleaning and sanitizing a fish tank is not all it is cracked up to be.

Horses require three things.

- Be very rich.
- Be very athletic.
- Give up nearly everything else. (First rule may apply a bit, but not much.)

Good news (mainly for adolescent men): It's a good way to meet girls.

Bad News: Remember the three rules above, and it may not be exactly what you had in mind.

Bad News: Horses die, and unlike Poochie-Woochie you cannot plant Divorce-me-Darling behind the rhubarb patch at the end of the garden.

Parrots, peacocks, pigs (guinea, human, or otherwise) and other fauna—well to each his own.

There are three problems with relationships with animals.

1. They do not feed themselves, and never will.
2. They are not lavatory friendly, and never will be.
3. They do not live as long as humans. (This does not include giant tortoises who are not good at touch-ie-feelie relationships, or elephants, who have other shortcomings as pets, certainly in Suburbia).

Get over it. What animals give back to any balanced human far outweighs their minor drawbacks.

Humans may be addressed as "pet," but not treated as such unless you both have a very complicated fantasy life.

ITS NOT A MATTER OF LIFE AND DEATH ETC

CARD GAMES AND BOARD GAMES

CHESS is only one game into which luck does not enter. Gamesmanship does as with so many other games.

A highly intelligent and well-known film star once sat down to play a lowly member of the film crew. After half a dozen moves his opponent acknowledged defeat. "Quite brilliant," he said and showed what he expected the next eight moves would be.

On a ten-week shoot the actor never won again.

A *draughts/checkers* shoe-in does not follow just because you were educated posh. Many of the world's great players honed their skills doing a five stretch for GBH.

Backgammon is a fascinating combination of skill and luck. Do not be seduced by beginners luck. You may well find you are being fattened for the kill by fate or your opponent.

Bridge is to many the king of card games, and socially—even today—a good game to know. Playing the game requires sharpness, short bursts of intense concentration, an ability to count and a certain deviousness. The structure of the game and the people it attracts allow time for short bursts of chat which can be intelligent, amusing, illuminating, or even gossip intensive. Warning: When you have learnt a few nuances it can become addictive.

Pontoon (twenty-one, *vingt et un* etc.) is only for the money. You need luck or special skill and, either way, nerves of steel. If your skill is counting cards and have a few learned skills you may even show a profit. The casinos are not thrilled by card counters and may suggest you leave. In such a case do not try your luck further down the Las Vegas strip, because the word will be out.

If on the other hand you have a run of amazing cards, you will be cosseted like a baby—free F&B in a nice suite overlooking the pool, even a little "company." Your "host" is only biding its time, because he wants to be there when the luck runs out—which it will.

There is a story that a group of math graduates from MIT actually did beat the system; it may be true, but it happened long ago, and although one is reputed to be a Wall Street whale he is not welcome in Las Vegas or Monte Carlo.

Poker has recently been deemed good TV fodder. Perhaps it is the chance to grandstand that attracts some posers and fancy dressers to provide eye candy. They add to the prurient delight of watching others lose money.

Playing poker is serious stuff at all levels. From now on you have no friend or ally; you are in a den of deception and double dealing.

That may sound like a description of big business manipulation; maybe poker is indeed a microcosm of Wall Street and that is its delight. Otherwise play Old Maid with your aunt—the one who took holy orders—and ask her not to cheat.

The basics of poker are well known:

- Do not frighten off the small punter with a big bet.

- Antagonize everyone a little. It gives you the upper hand.
- Do not reveal your hand unless necessary.
- Do not brag good luck or bad.
- If you bluff go all the way.
- Do not try to fill a straight.
- Count your winnings, but only once.
- Leave when broke.
- Do NOT borrow money from players or the pot if you cannot repay at once (i.e. NOW).
- Do NOT get up from the table immediately after a big win. (Bad luck and bad manners).
- Pretend drunk if you like but stay sober.
- Know when to hold, know when to fold.
- See *The Cincinnati Kid* and hear Kenny Rogers.
- Lose with grace.

One true cautionary tale:

An office poker school had developed; it had started as penny poker, to become quite serious. Someone in accounts whom everyone liked, each week declined the invitation to join in the fun.

"It's great. We all have a great time! We'll go over the rules for you!"

Eventually persuasion won over, and the school had a new sucker.

As a gesture of welcome, the newbie was offered first deal. Just as the lads were about to pick up their cards, he said quietly: "I like you fellows, but you should never play poker with strangers." He turned up his cards and left the table.

He had dealt himself four aces.

There are of course innumerable other games of cards and chance. Few have ever witnessed the end of a game of monopoly, there are canasta crazes occasionally, bezique is old-fashioned but fun, cribbage, and shove-ha'penny are fine pub games etc.

One unbreakable rule: If you are playing any game with small children it is your bounden duty to lose. Gracefully.

It's Not a Matter of Life and Death; It's Far More Important Than That

How about a gig where you work ninety minutes a week (unless you get a red card) you have three financial advisers, a personal manager and assistant, and your own geeks XI to tell you how wonderful you are, in case for a moment you forget.

You can get laid any time the mood takes you, and the media just says "Lucky bastard" and takes flattering pictures of your postcoital grin.

When that is over you get married and send your little darlings to Eton, Roedean, Miss Porter's, RADA, Juilliard, Yale, Oxford etc., and the media says "Well he's earned it. Remember his winning goal etc. etc."

In fact it's not quite that easy.

The first time six-year-old David Beckham put on an oversized pair of boots he did not dribble around three eight year olds and put the ball into the top left-hand corner of the net. It took a whole lot of effort, skill, luck and PR before the invitation to the Harry-Meghan ring-swap including some baby-kissing and an overdose of stupid questions.

Never underestimate the gulf between the good amateur and the average professional in any sport.

If you think that great day when you played eighteen holes in five over par means you are ready for the professional tour, you are smoking too many herbals.

It may be doubtful in the heat of the moment, but for us mere mortals sport is there to be enjoyed.

Team games if social are great for the inept, and lack of skill can be hidden in the general hurly-burly of a game played without noticeable skill or scheme.

There is a well-known writer who had his own cricket team, because it was his way to be sure of getting a game. Note: *If you wish for even a modicum of success in any amateur sport, brush up on your gamesmanship. Just saying.*

Croquet, deemed quite wrongly by some to be played by only ladies of a certain age, is great fun and requires little skill or practice for the duffer. It is also the most vicious, spiteful game ever devised. Many a vicarage tea party was in days of yore conducted in stony silence after polite battle on the croquet lawn.

Snooker, pool, darts, tennis and other court games can be very deceptive. The overweight apparent drunk may be able to stand in the center of the squash court and distribute the ball at will, exhausting his opponent while not even breaking a sweat. The man in the worn-out gym shoes may well have a laser serve.

Golf is loved by many, but it can sometimes turn normal rational beings into megalomaniac snobs. Perhaps it is the enormous amount of land they demand for their chosen sport.

If you've watched darts on the television it would seem none slimmer than an overweight Shetland pony is allowed to compete. Yet the throwing action is that of a brain surgeon.

No game is worth playing unless it is worth playing badly. (**Dick Clement**)

SPORTING DOS AND DO NOTS

Sadly what follows rarely applies to professionals.

- Brag about how badly you play, then, if you do win, you really are Cock of the Walk.
- If you are really unsure of your standing and wish to avoid humiliation, go with any variation of the sprained wrist.
- Do not lose your temper. No one made you play. You are there to have fun.
- Do not dispute rules or decisions. (See above).
- Do not play for money unless you have a very deliberate motive—that might include revenge or put-down. In that case be very sure you are going to win or lose if that is your intention. Collecting or paying can be very awkward (but great fun for the wrong reasons).
- Do not jump over the tennis net in victory unless you are sure you will make it.
- Do not bury your tongue in the mouth of your partner, particularly if any significant other is present.
- Do not let your little angels play any team game where everyone, win or lose, is given a cup or other token. Playing any sport or game is about losing as well as winning. So get used to it.

There are few who play any sport at any level who do not have that golden moment, that split second in time when body and mind are in harmony and the ball lands on the green and rolls into the hole, the ace service has the opponent's racket swishing fresh air, or ball hits bat and sails into the wild blue yonder or the well-defended goal.

And that is why they play the game. (**Chris Berman - ESPN**)

THREE THINGS YOU SHOULD NEVER DO

- Never eat in a restaurant called "Mum's."
- Never play cards with a man called "Ace."
- Never buy a computer from a man called "Chips."

Have a great life.

ABOUT THE AUTHOR

Born and educated in England and France, David Norton speaks English, French, Spanish and some American. He worked in several European countries as a commercial TV producer for various major international advertising agencies, winning the Golden Lion international prize for best cinema commercial. He has written commissioned comedy scripts, notably for top rated TV sitcom *Robin's Nest*, a spin off from the show that became *Three's Company* in the USA. He also wrote and produced industrial theater for clients such as Campbell's Soups, as well as launching for the United Kingdom such products as Foster's Draft Lager and Budweiser. He married into the United States and has continued to work in production for feature films, commercials, music videos, TV and documentaries. He has just coproduced a series on Viennese composers, currently being shown on SKY TV (UK) and thirty other countries. He lives in Miami with his family, which includes two cats, and is currently finishing his fourth book, a novel.

www.ingramcontent.com/pod-product-compliance
Lightning Source LLC
Chambersburg PA
CBHW031408250726
48656CB00002B/589